Alexander Hener

Credit Risk Management in the Automotive Industry

AF800049

GABLER EDITION WISSENSCHAFT

Alexander Hener

Credit Risk Management in the Automotive Industry

Structuring of loan and lease securitizations as integrative solution

With a foreword by Prof. Dr. Johannes Schneider

Deutscher Universitäts-Verlag

Bibliografische Information Der Deutschen Bibliothek
Die Deutsche Bibliothek verzeichnet diese Publikation in der Deutschen Nationalbibliografie; detaillierte bibliografische Daten sind im Internet über <http://dnb.ddb.de> abrufbar.

Dissertation Katholische Universität Eichstätt, 2004

1. Auflage März 2005

Alle Rechte vorbehalten
© Deutscher Universitäts-Verlag/GWV Fachverlage GmbH, Wiesbaden 2005

Lektorat: Brigitte Siegel / Nicole Schweitzer

Der Deutsche Universitäts-Verlag ist ein Unternehmen von
Springer Science+Business Media.
www.duv.de

Das Werk einschließlich aller seiner Teile ist urheberrechtlich geschützt. Jede Verwertung außerhalb der engen Grenzen des Urheberrechtsgesetzes ist ohne Zustimmung des Verlags unzulässig und strafbar. Das gilt insbesondere für Vervielfältigungen, Übersetzungen, Mikroverfilmungen und die Einspeicherung und Verarbeitung in elektronischen Systemen.

Die Wiedergabe von Gebrauchsnamen, Handelsnamen, Warenbezeichnungen usw. in diesem Werk berechtigt auch ohne besondere Kennzeichnung nicht zu der Annahme, dass solche Namen im Sinne der Warenzeichen- und Markenschutz-Gesetzgebung als frei zu betrachten wären und daher von jedermann benutzt werden dürften.

Umschlaggestaltung: Regine Zimmer, Dipl.-Designerin, Frankfurt/Main

Gedruckt auf säurefreiem und chlorfrei gebleichtem Papier

ISBN-13:978-3-8244-8287-0 e-ISBN-13:978-3-322-81917-8
DOI: 10.1007/978-3-322-81917-8

This thesis is dedicated to my family and to Arianne.

Foreword

When Alexander Hener started to work on this thesis three years ago, he may not have anticipated today's relevance of his research. The importance is for example reflected in the first asset-backed securities of underlying German auto finance contracts in November 2004, which has been structured by Volkswagen Financial Services. As result of the True-Sale Initiative fostered by the Kreditanstalt für Wiederaufbau more such transactions can be expected in the future. In this context Mr. Hener analyzes an intuitive question with relevance not only for German captives: which particular contracts from a pool of finance or lease contracts should be securitized in an ABS transaction?

The author first analyzes the reasons why portfolios in particular of automotive captives tend to be inefficiently priced. He sets out in detail different interest groups and potential conflicts in auto finance and lease, and suggests securitization as an integrative solution. Taking the issuer's point of view a framework is developed which suggests a decision for each contract as to whether it is to be assigned to an ABS transaction. Among other the framework models regulatory capital arbitrage, return on equity and return on risk-adjusted capital optimization.

For such an approach the underlying risks, in particular credit risk, must be modeled. With this purpose in mind the feasibility of various credit risk models in the industry context is extensively examined. Both the credit risk model and the securitization framework are then implemented and parameterized. The empirical study employs the subportfolio of a German captive and indicates that the suggested approach is feasible in practice. It can also be scaled to larger portfolios.

The research will be of value to both academia and practitioners with interest in securitization transactions of lease and finance contracts. From an academic point of view the author offers a significant and well-founded contribution to the issue of structuring ABS transactions. In addition to that, the suggestion of an applicable credit risk model should be of interest for practitioners involved with quantitative credit risk management. Of special interest in particular to the automotive industry is the analysis of how conflicts of interest between industrial companies and their captives can be handled.

For the reasons set out I am of the opinion that the approach developed herein integrates relevant theoretical and practical issues. I hope that this book will be accessed by a large and interested audience and initiate future research on applied issues of structuring ABS.

Prof. Dr. Johannes Schneider

Acknowledgements

This thesis would not have been possible without the gratuitous support of many people, and I must apologize in advance to anyone I might have left out. Most of all, I would like to express my gratitude to my doctoral advisor, Prof. Johannes Schneider, from the Catholic University of Eichstätt-Ingolstadt. Despite his many activities as dean of the Ingolstadt School of Management he has given me guidance and supervision to complete this thesis.

I am also indebted to Professor Gholamreza Nakhaeizadeh, my second advisor, and my colleagues in the Risk Group of the RIC/AM department at the DaimlerChrysler Research Center in Ulm. The practical experiences gained in the fields of data mining and risk management during my three years at the Research Center have broadened my horizons and are indispensable for my future career. Gratitude belongs as well to our project partners at DC Services and the DC Bank for giving me the opportunity to experience the applications of and the potential for credit risk management in automotive captive organizations.

My special thanks go to Professors Anthony Saunders, Edward Altman and Kose John of the Stern School of Business who took the time to discuss the relationship between regulatory and economic capital with me. Professor Ian Giddy of the same institution shared his experiences in the field of asset backed securities with me. I am also especially indebted to Professor Saunders for sponsoring me during my Stern visit in spring 2004. Of course, this visit would not have been possible without the gratuitous support of Professor Gholamreza Nakhaeizadeh.

I would like to thank Professor Heinrich Puschmann for fruitful discussions on the different optimization problems, and Dr. Thorsten Wingenroth for the review of the manuscript.

Alexander Hener

Contents

List of Figures

List of Tables

Chapter 1

Introduction

Overview and Purpose of Thesis

Most automotive banks and financial services throughout the world are not independent; instead they belong to a car manufacturing group. Examples of such captive finance companies are to be found at most car manufacturers: DaimlerChrysler Services at DaimlerChrysler, GMAC at General Motors or VW Financial Services at Volkswagen. As part of a parent company, management at such institutions has to focus on both typical banking and, in addition to that, manufacturer-induced objectives. In contrast to independent financial institutions, this may lead to different or even contradictory signals.

Manufacturing groups are devoted to shareholder value maximization, with special emphasis on sales growth and customer detention. The sales focus is due to factors influencing profits which are important but hard to quantify. In particular, in the automotive industry production processes are quite inflexible. Capacity reduction or even production stops come at enormous costs which are, however, difficult to measure. Sales also serve to avoid obsolescence and wearing down of the vehicles. The implied pressure to sell vehicles becomes obvious in such catch phrases as "move the metal" or put the "steel on the road".

By contrast, the business of banks is dealing with risks, with the goal of an optimal risk-return management. This includes the proper measurement and pricing of the risks taken on, e.g. in vehicle finance and lease contracts. From the perspective of auto bank management, the manufacturer's notion of using the financial institution as a sales channel can lead to additional constraints, or even be averse to risk-return considerations. Regarding credit risks, for example, risk-based pricing would necessitate calculating individual risk-adjusted premia based on the contract's risk contribution to the portfolio. However, individual rates are usually not observed in countries such as Germany.[1] An especially striking example where interests between the manufacturing and the banking sphere collide are uniform zero interest finance or lease contracts.

Captive financial institutions can deal with the problem of mispriced risks in their portfolio in three ways, as displayed in figure 1.1. These approaches are of two kinds: approaches through which the risk is passed on to the market, and those where the risk is kept within the group (so called pass-back). Under the latter approaches, risk measurement and management at the captive's level is restricted, and risks are implicitly covered by the group. This approach is certainly prone to criticism from the banking perspective.

Whereas the negligence of risks is an implicit pass back approach, internal payments make the risk transfer explicit. Such transfer payments serve to equalize the risks taken on by the captive which are not reflected in the customer rates. This calls for a two-step approach involving the modeling and measurement of the contractual risks. First, impulses conflicting with bank management goals must be traced back to a non-financial unit. As an example, marketing or sales units justify zero-finance contracts, which should be at odds with the intuition of risk-based pricing, by market conditions. These units are then charged internally with the difference between contractual and risk-adjusted interest. This approach is preferable to ignoring the risks, since it requires an integrated view of the risks involved.

Apart from passing back the risk to, or rather keeping it within, the group, the risk can also be passed on to the markets by means of securitization. Under this portfolio management approach, a security whose payments are based on those of an underlying pool is created. This pool can be generated by bundling finance and lease contracts. Securitizations are highly complex transactions and call for a thorough analysis of the underlying risks. Yet, they are currently

[1] Limited risk adjustments are possible even under standardized contract conditions. An example are higher downpayments at contract initiation which reduce overall risk at the cost of income from interest.

in wide-spread use. Although the motivation for securitization is largely refinancing, practitioners agree that the future management of credit risk by means of asset-backed securities is currently under examination. Since the internal payment approach may not be viable due to opposition from within the group, passing the risk on is very likely the only feasible approach to portfolio management if risks are not to be ignored.

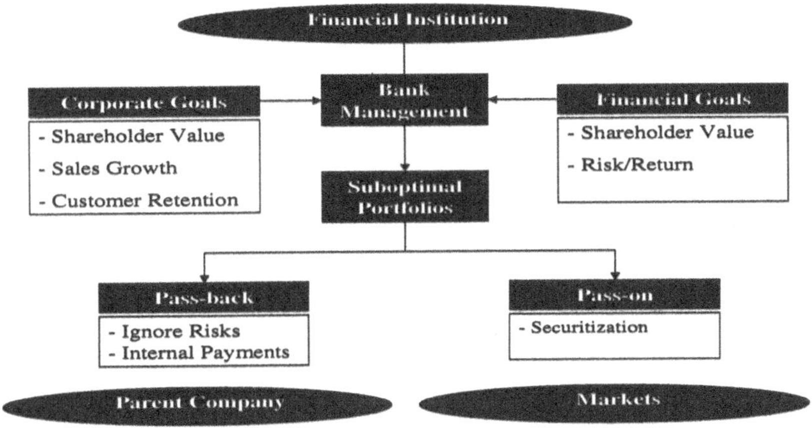

Figure 1.1: Solutions for Conflicts at Automotive Banks

The purpose of this thesis is to develop a framework for passing on credit risks by securitization. It is innovative in two regards. First, it suggests a formal model for the construction of the underlying of an asset backed security from the issuer's point of view. An optimization problem is given for the choice of contracts to be securitized from a portfolio. Among the motivations to be modeled is regulatory capital arbitrage. The question of which contracts precisely to choose for such a transaction has, to the author's best knowledge, thus far not been researched. This observation holds for both captives and traditional non-captive banks.

The securitization framework requires a credit risk model: this model must, in particular, take default dependencies and loss rate volatility into account. The second innovation in the thesis is the analysis and implementation of such a model tailored to the specific requirements of the automotive industry. The implementation of this model makes extensive use of two unique data sets for vehicle residual values and finance contracts at a large German captive.

Literature Review

Literature on risk management in the context of manufacturing groups is generally scarce, and tends to focus on those market risks of importance for the production process. Examples include energy or currency markets, whereas credit risk is typically neglected.[2] Although the general literature on credit risk modeling is vast and constantly growing, practical aspects are often neglected.

Addressing the specific requirements in the automotive industry, the author is aware of only three sources. The first is Beyer (1996), which examines approaches to managing the residual value of leasing contracts by hedging on residual value indices. The author suggests option-based strategies similar to those applied for market risks. Since such options on residual value indices are currently not traded, this approach is in spite of its academic merit not feasible in practice.[3] Moreover, only residual value risk is analyzed whereas credit risk is not further considered.

Riess (2003) also focuses on residual value risk in lease contracts. He suggests a model to derive the loss distribution at contract end, taking into account both residual value volatility and the probability that the customer decides to buy the car. Correlations are modeled without further specifications by amortization rules, default risk is again not included. Closest in spirit to this thesis is the approach in Schmit (2002). This paper uses a CreditRisk+ framework to calculate expected and unexpected losses for different lease portfolios, including automotive leases. Although the paper provides interesting empirical results, there are two significant differences with regard to the modeling approach in this thesis. First, to model loss rate volatility, a Monte Carlo simulation is used. Given the potential problems involved in simulations, however, this thesis uses instead an alternative analytical solution. Second, Schmit (2002) analyzes

[2](See Gebhardt and Mansch, 2001).

[3]Residual value indices, however, have been introduced, an example being Schwacke's Automobil-Forecast-Index ("F-SAX").

portfolio risk measures only, whereas for the purpose of this thesis individual risk contributions are required.

Outline of Thesis

This thesis contains eight chapters. After this introduction, the next chapter analyzes in more detail the general situation in the automotive industry and the traditional stakeholders and interest groups. In the third chapter follows a discussion of general and industry specific modeling elements. Based on a survey of different credit risk models and the requirements, a specific model, CreditRisk+, is chosen for implementation. The model, its extensions and implementations are described in the following chapter four. Chapter four also contains an introduction of the regulatory model. Credit risk management, in particular the calculation of risk contributions to portfolio risk measures, is the topic of chapter four. The calculation of both portfolio risk measures and of risk contributions are examined both in general and when CreditRisk+ is employed as credit risk model.

Chapter six contains the core of this thesis. Based on the portfolio risk measures and risk contributions, a framework for the construction of the underlying of an securitization transaction is developed. Different motivations are modeled and presented in an optimization framework that can easily be implemented. These motivations include among other regulatory capital arbitrage and the optimization of return on equity and return on risk-adjusted capital.[4] Further inputs to the framework include regulatory capital, which is discussed in detail. The chapter also contains a thorough discussion of securitization transactions and their usage at automotive captives.

The following chapter describes the implementation of two of the motivations introduced in chapter six: regulatory capital arbitrage and minimization of regulatory capital. The optimization employs a unique data set of a large German captive. The final chapter summarizes and concludes with an outlook for future research. Detailed computations as well as variable declarations and abbreviations are provided in appendices.

---

[4]See section 6.1.2 for definitions.

Final Remarks

Not only does this thesis give support for projects at the DaimlerChrysler Research&Technology Center, Ulm (Germany), it also profits from them. On the one hand, portfolio optimization and selection are explicit purposes of the business strategy at DaimlerChrysler Services ("DCS"). This goal and its implications for DaimlerChrysler R&T are reflected in different projects, an example being the suggested long-term project on integrated information mining. Such approaches to portfolio management call for, after a careful general formulation of management purposes, a formal framework. In this regard, the thesis suggests and implements different potential purposes. In addition, credit risk management at DCS will generally be advanced by the choice and implementation of a credit risk model as a necessary prerequisite for any portfolio management approach. On the other hand, especially the participation in two projects focusing on risks in car fleet management allowed the author to obtain valuable insights on residual value volatilities.

Chapter 2

The Automotive Industry

2.1 Relevance of the Industry and of the Captive Financial Companies

The automotive has changed the world more than any prophet.

Joseph Schumpeter

The importance of the automobile, and of the automotive industry, results from its role as both a vehicle for transportation and also as an economic factor.[1] With regard to the former role, it is individual mobility which is of most importance for automotive financing and leasing and which, in 1999, accounted for a significant 80% of motorized traffic in Germany. This amount seems to be spread equally between professional and leisure-time individual traffic.[2]

Concerning the role as an economic factor, the production process is complex: this is especially true with respect to the added value and the intersections with other industries.[3] Such intersections exist to the refining industry, maintenance companies and other companies

[1]There is no unique definition for the automotive industry. Here, following Diez and Brachat (2001), p. 43, it is used as a summarizing term for all companies which are mainly concerned with the production, marketing, maintenance as well as recycling of automobiles.

[2](See Diez and Brachat, 2001, pp. 25–26).

[3](See Diez and Brachat, 2001, p. 46).

providing services such as insurance. The importance is further reflected by the size of the corporations involved, as indicated by their production and sales volumes. As the magazine "Finanztest" noted in August 2002, roughly 55 million passenger cars and small transporters were sold worldwide in 2001. Of these, the number of licenses in Europe alone soared to 14.8 million in 2000, whereas in Japan the number of licenses stayed constant at 4.26 million. The increases were however not equally distributed across the European countries. For example, sales decreased in Germany to 3.33 million, which was offset by sales boosts in France and the United Kingdom. This in part positive trend despite decreased consumer confidence in that year indicates the importance placed on mobility.[4]

Regarding other economic indicators, a study of the United Nations Conference on Trade and Development showed that among the hundred largest "economic entities" are 29 transnational corporations, seven of which are car manufacturers. In Germany the value added of the automotive industry amounts to approximately one fifth of the gross national product. The industry supports more than five million employees, accounting for roughly 14% of the German workforce.[5] Also of economic importance especially in Germany are the taxes associated with automobiles, such as taxes on fuel, value added taxes or vehicle taxes.

There are currently two trends in the automotive industry, the integration of vehicle and communication technology and manufacturer concentration. The first trend is motivated by the pressure on the manufactures to provide distinct products despite the industry-wide convergence of engineering, design and production quality. With respect to concentration, in 1999 alone there were 543 mergers and acquisition activities throughout the industry. In fact, some forecasts predict that only seven or fewer independent manufacturers will be left at some point in the future, and forecasts are similar for the subcontractors. As noted by "Finanztest", the umbrella organization of the German subcontractors CLEPA predicts a decline from what are today 8,000 subcontractors to 150 in 2008.

---

[4]"Credit" noted in June 2002 that the contracts might also have provided special incentives to the customers, de facto decreasing the manufacturers' profits.

[5](See Diez and Brachat, 2001, p. 47).

Manufacturer	Production (m Vehicles)	Sales (bn EUR)	Profit (bn EUR)	Employees	Captive
General Motors	7.00	188.0	0.6	350,000	GMAC Bank
Ford	6.90	172.0	-5.5	115,000	Ford Financial
Toyota	5.50	110.0	10.0	215,000	Toyota Financial Services
Volkswagen	5.10	88.0	4.4	322,000	VW Financial Services
Renault	4.70	36.3	1.0	140,000	RCI Banque
DaimlerChrysler	4.59	153.0	1.3	372,000	DC Bank
Peugeot	3.10	52.5	2.7	192,500	PSA Finance
Honda	2.66	58.5	2.7	114,000	Honda Bank
Nissan	2.45	50.0	3.5	125,000	RCI Banque
Fiat	2.00	58.0	-0.8	224,000	Fiat Bank

Table 2.1: Car Manufacturers in 2001 (Sources: "Finanztest", August 2002 and http://www.autobanken.de)

Table 2.1 sets out the largest international manufacturers in 2001 with four business indicators and the affiliated captive finance companies in Germany.[6] The figures indicate both the concentration and the economic importance of the industry. The former is likely to increase, especially since the cooperation between Nissan and Renault as well as between Fiat and General Motors ("GM") are likely to be extended. Currently, Renault owns 44% of Nissan, and GM owns 20% of Fiat.

2.2 Risk Management in Industry and Commerce

The evolvement of risk management in industrial and other commercial companies since the 1970ies has been strongly influenced by two developments.[7] These were the fundamental changes in the markets for goods and services, which were partly due to the globalization,

[6]Although in Germany, the local captives are often listed as "bank", they usually belong to the international "financial services" division of the manufacturer.

[7](See Gebhardt and Mansch, 2001, pp. 1–4).

Risk Types	
Credit risk	Country and transfer risk
Market risk	Interest rate risk
Liquidity risk	Operational risk
Legal risk	Reputational risk

Table 2.2: Risk Types in Banking (Source: BIS (1997), p. 20)

and the rocketing volatilities of not only exchange and interest rates but also of commodity prices. As a result, it was no longer possible for such companies to focus exclusively on their core competencies, for example the development of new and innovative products or marketing campaigns. Instead, it became necessary to develop methods for active risk measurement and management. This trend was further enhanced by shareholder demands.

In the following sections, both the relevant risks and risk management techniques in general and specifically in the automotive industry are described. The first section gives an overview over the risks in classical banking.

2.2.1 Risks and Risk Management in Banking

The Basle Committee on Banking Supervision has classified the risks encountered in banking as described in table 2.2. These risk types are generic in the sense that definitions are not always clear cut, for example between market and interest rate risk. They should however include most sources of risk that may occur at financial institutions. Of special interest in the context of this dissertation is credit risk, which can be defined as follows:[8]

Definition 1 (Credit Risk) *Credit risk is defined as the degree of value fluctuations in debt instruments and derivatives due to changes in the underlying credit quality of borrowers and counterparties.*

[8](See Lopez and Saidenberg, 2000, p. 152).

Credit risk is the basic and classical risk involved in banking. However, there were few incentives especially for quantitative research until very recently.[9] The reasons for this negligence by both practitioners and theoreticians has been two-fold. First, other areas of risk management were more promising and pressing, most notably market risks. Public and academic interest in derivatives has for example been sparked by the affairs at Baring's or in Orange County. Furthermore, data availability has stood against quantitative credit risk modeling. Sufficient amounts of data were not available primarily due to the fact that credit risk evolves more slowly than market risk, which can be measured on a daily basis. Today, the data management and accumulation processes and the formal methods have improved, a trend which is furthered by regulatory influences.

A more subtle problem involved in credit risk is to find unique definitions of the relevant terms.[10] Proper definitions are not only of academic interest, as is for example indicated by the current discussion among regulators as to whether or not unexpected loss should contain expected losses. This discussion may topple the new capital regimen Basle II and thus has significant influence on all financial institutions concerned. In addition, the term unexpected loss itself is not used in connection with a unique risk measure. As an example, in Hirtle et al. (2001), p. 21, the unexpected loss refers to Value at Risk, but in Ong (1999), p. 112, it refers to the standard deviation.[11]

Also of interest is the question of whether both upward and downward potential should be considered as risk. In the context of this thesis, the term risk is restricted to the downward potential of a random variable, and credit risk is divided into default risk and spread risk.

---

[9]A notable exemption is the work of Prof. Edward I. Altman at New York University, whose research in the field dates back to the late 60.

[10]Moreover, the term credit risk itself can be misleading, implying that this type of risk can only occur in credit transactions.

[11]A survey of different risk measures for the unexpected loss is given in section 5.1.1. Expected loss is uniquely defined as the expected value of the loss distribution.

2.2.2 Risks in Industry and Commerce

A survey of the risks relevant in industrial and commercial companies is set out in figure 2.1. Corporate risks are all those risks which may lead to a temporal, qualitative or quantitative deterioration of production. These include strikes, machine or power failures. In the figure, the risks specific to the corporate finance units are depicted separately. Market risks can be divided into economic risks, which result from economic exposures, and consolidation risks. Consolidation risks arise in groups of companies and result from translation exposures. The latter are of relevance for the consolidation of financial statements across different currency areas. Gebhardt and Mansch (2001), p. 14, give an example of a company that hedges the impact of exchange rate risk on the assets to be consolidated on the balance sheet.

Economic risks can be separated into transaction risks, latent risks and competition risks. Transaction risks such as interest, commodity or exchange rate risks occur when future prices are volatile. By contrast, competition risks occur due to potential changes regarding the competitive environment. Finally, latent risks occur in connection with contingent exposures, for example when an industrial group makes a construction bid. Depending on whether the group wins the bid, a multitude of other risks can arise: if the bid is on a project in another currency zone, potential exchange rate risk is induced. Other risks in manufacturing and industry are credit, country, reputational and legal risks. Country risk refers to the dangers associated with economic, social and political environments, e.g. social turmoils, strikes or dispossession. Reputational risks arise from operational failures or the failure to comply with relevant laws and regulations, which leads to a decrease of the perceived reputation. This may, for example, result in higher refinancing rates, or loss of sales. Thirdly, legal risks are the dangers of unexpected changes in laws which affect current contracts or the reduced legal enforceability of contractual agreements.

As is the case for banking, all these risk types are generic. For example, exchange rate volatility may also induce competitive risk. A strong Euro both decreases the value of dollar-nominated income, and weakens the international competitiveness of European car manufacturers. Research so far has focused on market risks, and certain other risks such as country

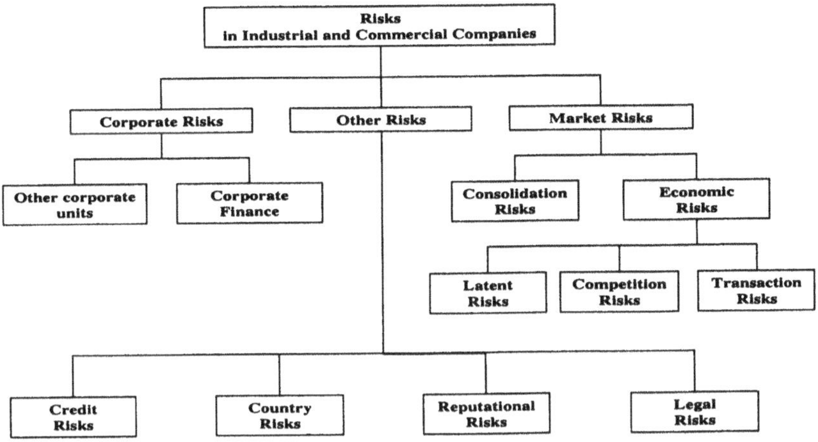

Figure 2.1: Risks in Industry and Commerce (Source: Gebhardt and Mansch (2001), p. 23)

risks.[12] This is mostly due to the problems involved in quantifying the other risk groups, especially in the field of corporate risks.

2.2.3 Risk Management in Industry and Commerce

Approaches to risk management in manufacturing and commerce are given in figure 2.2.[13] The three general approaches are either to adopt, to reject or to reduce risk. Whereas the adoption and the rejection of risks are exclusively ex ante methods, risk reduction may be either ex ante or ex post. It can be divided into five subgroups. First, a company can strive to reduce its potential losses, for example by improving machine maintenance. As an alternative, it might be desirable to transfer the risks, for which securitization is an example. Third, risk diversification is possible if different risks offset each other. These methods can be separated into those belonging to the corporate and those relevant for the financial sphere. Corporate diversification can be done by spreading activities across different products or different markets. Financial

[12]See for example Beyer (1996), Gebhardt and Mansch (2001) or Bühler (1998).

[13]For alternative classifications see Bühler (1998) or Beyer (1996).

diversification is usually done by appropriate financial instruments, which allow hedging exchange rate or commodity risks, for example. The other two general approaches, if available, are insurance and the creation of contingeny, i. e. capital, reserves.

In the context of this thesis, the focus lies on the risk reduction techniques of risk transfer and contingency reserves. With regard to the former, the securitization of loan and lease contracts is examined. Concerning the use of contingency reserves, both economic and regulatory capital are defined and implemented in the context of the securitization model in chapter 6.

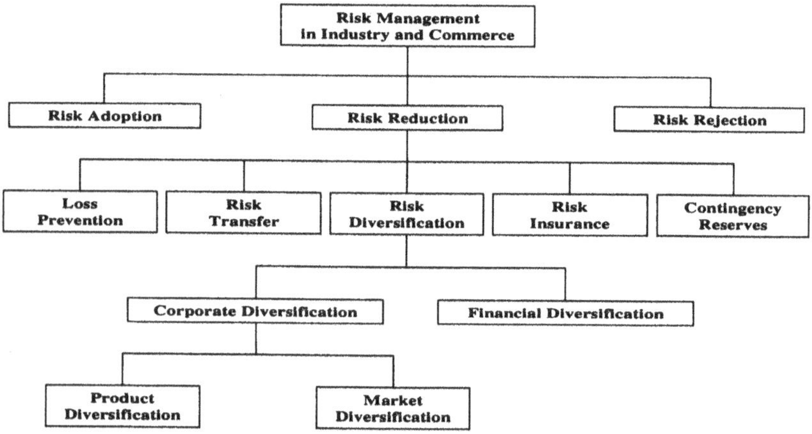

Figure 2.2: Risks Management in Industry and Commerce (Source: Gebhardt and Mansch (2001), p. 34)

2.2.4 Risks and Risk Management in the Automotive Industry

In some respects, banks have it easy when it comes to risk management.

Duncan Wood, ERisk

Risk management in the automotive industry is currently experiencing significant changes. As a representative example, in 2000 Ford hired former banker Freeman Wood to integrate the existing risk management groups, i.e. foreign exchange, interest rate, credit, commodity and insurance risk. For the future, risk measures are to be employed for capital allocation as well as performance evaluation.

In addition to what could be a general trend, changes might be enforced when regulating authorities are involved. For example, in Germany the regulator subordinates all banks, including affiliated financial institutions, under the new capital regime Basle II. The general idea behind Basle II, which is still in the pipeline, is to make legal capital requirements more risk sensitive, thus encouraging banks to explicitly consider risk issues when managing their portfolios. By contrast, Norden (2002) describes the captive of a German car producer where risk data are collected, but not used for the computation of risk-adjusted prices. Instead, due to sale arguments, an average flat rate is exploited to price in risk costs.

The specific structures of risk and risk management in the automotive industry result from the interdependencies between the areas finance/lease, manufacturing, and remarketing.[14] There are also many risks which occur irregularly, for example in the case of additional services or cross-country transactions. With regard to the risks involved, there is no difference between finance and lease contracts, although residual value risks should play a more important role in lease contracts.

Generic approaches to risk management in the automotive industry are analyzed in Beyer (1996). The author differentiates between approaches for risk prophylaxis, risk reduction, and risk compensation. Risk prophylaxis approaches do not influence or transfer risks, instead attempting to prepare for its effects. Such approaches can be divided into risk rejection and risk precaution. Examples of the latter are risk-based pricing, write-offs in advance or risk diversification. By contrast, risk reduction techniques seek to influence the risk directly. Examples for this approach are increased downpayments, used car leasing or revolving lease contracts, where the original lease interval is split into smaller time periods.[15] Finally, risk compensation methods try to compensate ex post for the case of losses. Examples are residual value and credit insurance, forfeiting and risk transfers from the manufacturer to the dealer.

---

[14](See Beyer, 1996).

[15]Downpayments on the other hand decrease the finance or lease amount.

In particular from the captive's point of view, however, a risk management classification should take into account the opaque structure of car manufacturers. Assuming that conflicting goals inside such an organization exist between the corporate and the financial sphere, affiliated financial organizations can be expected to hold a significant part of their portfolios at suboptimal conditions from a financial perspective.[16] Thus, risk management should focus on the ex post management of existing contracts. An appropriate classification can distinguish between two general approaches with different implications regarding the role of the captive and the allocation of the risks.[17] The first approach is to pass the risk back to the parent company by neglecting risk measurement and management, relying on the group's financial potential. From this point of view, the financial institution is regarded as a non-autonomous part of the distribution channel, not as an asset lender. Alternatively, risk can be transferred or shared by internal transfer payments. This is a two-step approach, where conflicting impulses are initially traced back to a non-financial unit, which is then charged with the difference between realized and risk-adjusted charges. Apart from passing back the risk to, or rather keeping it within, the group, risk can also be passed on to the markets by securitization. This vehicle is already in extensive use today, removing credit risk at least partially, for example by means of asset-backed securities.

2.3 Stakeholders in the Automotive Industry

2.3.1 Classical Stakeholders and Captive Finance Companies

Demnach ist zu empfehlen, die Ertragsziele aus Finanzdienstleistungen den Kundenbindungszielen unterzuordnen.

Heinz W. Kiefer

Traditionally, stakeholder analysis in the automotive industry focuses on interest groups along the value chain. There are three such groups: subcontractors, manufacturers, and deal-

[16] For the different stakeholders at a car manufacturer see section 2.3.

[17] (See figure 1.1, p. 3).

ers, who are in charge of sales and maintenance. All three are heterogenous with regard to company size and the international, national or even local focuses.[18] For the financing and leasing business, subcontractors are of less importance, as an additional focus is placed on the private, corporate or governmental customer instead. Although from this point of view the shareholders' interests are not implicitly analyzed, they can be assumed to be incorporated in the manufacturer's goals.

Interests common to all three groups include the demand for individual financing solutions, fast and informal credit decisions and a comprehensive product range. Key issues in car financing from the dealers' perspective are customer loyalty, improved sales volumes, which can be induced by improved customer proximity, high transaction volumes and the possibility to better plan used car sales and enhance the capacity utilization of the garages.[19]

In contrast, from the manufacturer's point of view it is of importance to generate profit all along the value chain. Of special interest is the observation that approximately 50% of sales and as much as 70% of earnings are made after the manufacturing process. Sales, and thus earnings, are generated not only by providing financial services but also by selling after-sales products and services, e.g. spare parts and maintenance, mobility services such as fleet management and other services such as recycling.[20] Another pivotal issue are the huge costs implied in adjusting production volumes. This induces an urge on the manufacturer's part to "move the metal" or put the "steel on the road".

From this follows a natural dichotomy between the dealerships and a captive financial company. However, there seems to be a consensus that in the customer's view, financial services are merely an additional service in the context of car purchase.[21] This leads to the conclusion that, particularly in a competitive market, the customer value of the package car plus financial service should not be reduced, for example by charging risk-adjusted interest.[22] The institution

[18](See Diez and Brachat, 2001, p. 48).

[19](See Kiefer, 2001, p. 301).

[20](See Kiefer, 2001, p. 305).

[21](See for example Kiefer, 2001, p. 303).

[22]Diez and Brachat (2001), p. 66, analyze the main drivers for construction of the distribution channel, which has significant impact on the relative power of the dealers. They use only one risk-related determinant, which is

financing the vehicle purchase is thus not perceived as an independent unit of the distribution channel. Instead, it should be able to adapt to customer needs and, in general, exercise few controls over the dealers. In this sense, it serves only as sales support unit, which should also be willing to take on unrewarded risk to achieve this goal.[23]

Astoundingly, captive finance companies are not necessarily perceived as superior to independent loan or lease providers from the dealers' perspective. In Germany for example, this is reflected by the Dealer Financing Satisfaction Index of the Forschungsstelle Automobilwirtschaft in Bamberg.[24] One of the main results has been that AKB Bank, an independent lease and finance institution which also offers non-vehicle related services, obtained a better score than the manufacturer-owned banks in most cases. The observation that non-captive finance institutions can be governed by banking principles and still successfully compete indicates that such principles can be applied to captives. Moreover, they should be applied to ensure proper risk levels, e.g. with regard to the residual value risk arising from lease contracts. And finally they must applied given the increasing influence of the regulator.

2.3.2 The Regulator as Additional Stakeholder

In God we trust, all others must bring data.

Anonymous

Apart from the stakeholders discussed above, regulatory requirements can be of importance. Events such as the oil futures debacle at German Metallgesellschaft have alarmed the legislators. In Germany, for example, the "Gesetz zur Kontrolle und Transparenz im Unternehmensbereich" (Law on Control and Transparency in the Corporate Sector, "KonTraG") has been introduced. This law requires companies to install a corporate and financial risk monitoring system which must be able to detect in advance any developments which might

the potential transfer of residual value risk to the dealer.

[23](See Kiefer, 2001, p. 304).

[24]The motivation behind this study is to provide a measure which describes the satisfaction of independent car dealers, as the interface between manufacturer and customer, with the financing institution. The study is performed irregularly, in 1999 it captured the comments of 1218 car dealers, see Meinig (2000).

endanger the continued existence of the company in the future. It is further required to monitor risks throughout the group and has to be audited by a chartered accountant. Requirements include a comprehensive reporting and controlling system.[25]

Financial institutions may fall under local jurisdiction regarding credit risk, especially given the trend to extend the product offerings from finance and lease contracts to deposits, credit cards or insurances contracts. Though the regulatory requirements may vary locally, they tend to be based on the recommendations from the Bank of International Settlements ("BIS") in Basle.

The BIS was established in 1930 in the context of the reparation payments imposed on Germany in connection with the Treaty of Versailles. However, the focus quickly turned to the general issue of international cooperation between central banks and other agencies in pursuit of monetary and financial stability. Today, the BIS's main tasks include the provision of a forum for central bank cooperation, classical banking functions, and, in particular, emergency financing.[26]

Of special interest to banks is the research carried out and formulation of recommendations aimed at strengthening the international financial system. The latter task included the development of the 1988 Basle Capital Accord on regulatory capital requirements, which is currently under revision. The Accord was developed by the Committee on Banking Supervision, in short the Committee, which was established in 1974. Its members are representatives of the central banks and, if necessary, of other supervisory authorities. In addition to the Accord, the Committee formulates and publishes "broad supervisory standards ... in the expectation that individual authorities will take steps to implement them through detailed arrangements".[27]

An objective the Committee has been dedicated to is ensuring that no banking institution evades adequate supervision. Generally, banking supervision is defined as ensuring that banks operate in a safe and sound manner and that they hold capital and reserves sufficient to support the risks that arise in their business. It is argued that "the banking system plays a central role

---

[25](See § 91 II AktG).

[26]For more information on the BIS see http://www.bis.org.

[27]For more information on the Committee see http://www.bis.org/bcbs/.

in making payments and mobilizing and distributing savings", and thus, "effective supervision ... is an essential component of a strong economic environment".[28] The envisioned purpose of banking supervision is then to provide the public good financial stability in accordance with an appropriate macroeconomic policy. Macroeconomic policy, but also infrastructure elements, are not under supervisory responsibility.

To make these goals operational, the regulator can, for example, strive to reduce the losses of depositors or other creditors or generally foster an efficient and competitive banking system providing good services at reasonable costs.[29] In this regard, it is also important to note that, first, there is a positive relationship between the level of risk tolerance and the costs of financial intermediation: that is, extensive supervision may distort financial allocations and hinder innovations. Second, the purpose of financial stability is not to avoid bank defaults. Instead, failures are seen as a natural part of risk-taking.

The Committee differentiates various types of risks a bank is facing. Of these, credit risk is the potential failure of a counterparty to perform according to a contractual arrangement and lies at the heart of this thesis. Potential conflicts between a credit risk management as required by the regulator and the other stakeholders' goals may then arise in many aspects. In spite of the fact that the Committee's publications are merely recommendations and the Committee has no formal legal authority, the specifications are usually translated into national law, and manufacturer-owned financial institutions often fall under regulatory discretion.

2.3.3 Conflict of Interest

The potential conflicts between credit risk management on the one hand and traditional automotive finance on the other are best analyzed by examining the "Principles for the Management of Credit Risk".[30] These are seventeen principles published by the Committee in 2000. They serve as basic requirements on credit policy for the national regulators. The principles are di-

[28](See BIS, 1997, p. 8).

[29](See BIS, 1997, pp. 8–9). General requirements for a credit risk regulatory framework are described in Hirtle et al. (2001).

[30](See BIS, 2000).

vided into five groups, relating to credit risk environment, the credit decision, administration of contracts, credit risk control and regulatory surveillance.

Potential conflicts can arise in particular with respect to the principles related to the environment and the credit decision. The first group of principles requires that the board of directors periodically review and approve the credit risk strategy and the credit risk policies. This strategy should be based on a thorough understanding of the risks inherent in all products and is to be implemented by senior management. When applying these principles to an automotive captive finance company, the discussion in section 2.3.1 implies problems: the board of directors must balance additional goals that are not risk related and which may override risk management considerations. The second group refers to the soundness of the credit granting process. Principles four to seven in this group demand a clearly established process for approving new credits based on well-defined criteria. Moreover, it requires credit limits at the level of individual borrowers and counterparties, and extensions to be made on an arm's-length basis. The latter necessitates that the terms and conditions of credits to related companies and individuals not be more favorable than credit granted to non-related borrowers under similar circumstances.[31] Again, the results from section 2.3.1 indicate potential conflicts between sales and risk considerations.

Given the potentially contradictory impulses and taking into account the regulator as a new stakeholder leaves a captive financial institution at the center of a number of conflicting interests. This is depicted in figure 2.3 for the different parties shareholders, customer, dealer, manufacturer, and regulator. Note that the dealers do not always belong to the group. In this case, they can be expected to advocate their specific goals even more fiercely.

2.4 Summary

There are a multitude of risks involved in manufacturing and commerce, including and beyond most of those occurring in the financial industry. Many of these risks are difficult to quantify, e.g. corporate risks such as strikes. Research on the manufacturing industry has been limited,

[31](See BIS, 2000, p. 12).

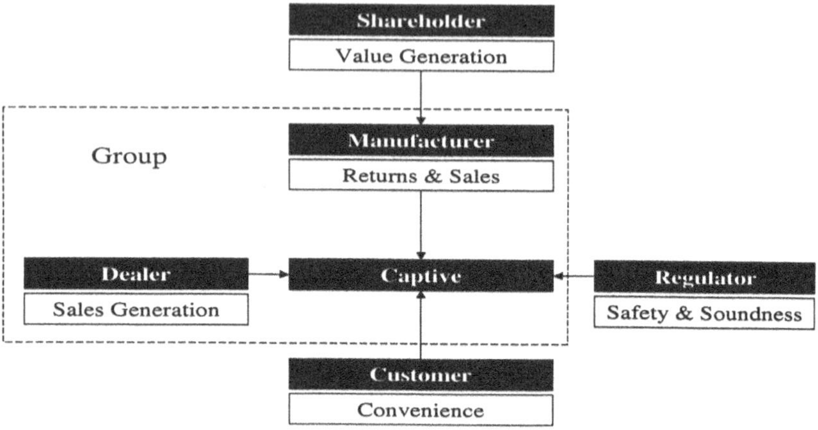

Figure 2.3: Interest Groups in Car Financing

as opposed to the financial industry, and usually targeted market risks.

It has further been shown that manufacturing groups comprise different internal and external interest groups. Different motivations may enforce behavior in contradiction to financial principles regarding, among other, credit risk management. This can lead to suboptimal portfolios from a risk-return point of view. There have, however, been changes recently in particular due to the increasing influence of the regulator on many financial captives.

Building on the research that has been done for the financial industry, the focus of this thesis is on the management of credit risk at captive finance companies. It deals specifically with the question of which subportfolios should be securitized in an asset-backed security transaction from different perspectives. All these motivations are developed in a comprehensive formal framework.

Chapter 3

Credit Risk Models

Traditionally, credit risk management consisted of isolated approaches, often in the form of limit setting. Examples include limits on credit exposure in certain rating classes, regions or industries.[1] Yet for an integrated approach, credit risk models are necessary. The Bank for International Settlements ("BIS") describes no fewer than three general advantages of credit risk management based on quantitative models.[2] These begin with improvements in risk identification, measurement and management for the overall portfolio, especially insights into portfolio-specific risk drivers such as concentration risks. Second, the possibility to model structural changes is important. Such changes not only include credit cycles, they also encompass other relevant macro-economic shifts. Finally, explicit quantitative modeling can lead to improvements in data collection, quality, and management and of credit processes in general.

The purpose of this chapter is to derive a suggestion for a credit risk model applicable at a captive. In the first section, the general requirements for a credit risk model in automotive finance and lease are analyzed. The second section presents a discussion of general elements of quantitative credit risk models. Based on the results from previous two sections, section three concludes with the suggestion of a model feasible in this setting.

---

[1](See Wilde, 1997a, p. 29).

[2]See BIS (1999b), p. 3, or Matten (2000), p. 148.

3.1 Model Requirements in the Automotive Industry

3.1.1 Types of Products in Car Financing and Leasing

Contracts in car financing can be divided into finance, lease, and rent. Since the difference between the last two is not clear cut, especially in Anglo-Saxon countries, rent is summarized under leasing and neglected in the following.

Leasing

A lease can be generically defined as a contract granting utilization or occupation of an object during a specified period in exchange for rent without a transfer of ownership. The contract covers all the terms and conditions in relation to the transfer of usage and the repayment. In the automotive industry, leasing is popular in particular with commercial customers. In this field, three types of leasing can be differentiated: automobile leasing, services leasing including car fleet management, and leasing of company cars.[3]

Automobile leasing, as opposed to the purchase of a vehicle, often offers advantages with respect to taxes and capital commitment. Also, specifications can be used to customize the lease contract. These usually concern purchasing options, or the re-allocation of residual value risk, for example in the form of residual value or maximal usage guaranties on behalf of the customer. The second generic type, services leasing and car fleet management, allows the customer to source out, partly or wholly, maintenance and repair as well as the object management. Finally, the leasing of official cars can be seen as both a fiscally and financially attractive alternative to a raise in salary from the company's point of view.

Financing

Financing is used mainly by private customers, who oftentimes wish to exploit the subsided rates offered by the car manufacturers. There are five generic types of financing contracts.[4]

[3](See Kiefer, 2001, pg. 289).

[4](See Kiefer, 2001, pg. 293).

In standard contracts, the customer pays amortization and interest in fixed monthly payments. Second, finance contracts may include balloon payments, where the final payment is increased and foregoing payments are decreased. This kind of contracts might permit the customer to optionally obtain the vehicle before the agreed-upon end of the contract by an advanced and increased final payment. Third, finance contracts might allow for flexible payments in accordance with the business cycle of the customer. For example, a construction company might be more solvent in the summer time, when contractual payments are increased. In other seasons, they can be adjusted accordingly. Finally, there is start-up financing, where the payments are completely postponed, starting for example 90 days after the contract has been made.

The long term rent, as a special case of a finance contract, is frequently met with in the US and Great Britain, but not for example in Germany. This is due to legal reasons, since the lessor is generally obliged to provide substitutes for the rented object in the case of damage. The lessor is also responsible for repairs and maintenance.

Other contracts and outlook

Some practitioners perceive that the need for service leasing and financing contracts beyond the loan or lease payments will increase especially in the retail market. To provide a customer service which is as general as possible, captives strive to extend their product catalogue. This is motivated by cost synergies and an increased customer satisfaction.[5]

Examples for additional product offerings are insurances, not necessarily vehicle related, and deposit and investment products in general. "Spiegel-online" noted a particular example on August 15, 2002: according to the source, Skoda offered insurances which included a free insurance of the contract payments if the customers were laid off during the term of the contract. Deposit products are, for example, contracts where the customer can open a savings account which can be used to finance a vehicle at some point in the future. Investment products include retirement benefits and credit cards. For corporate customers, it seems likely that the trend for outsourcing, and hence service leasing, will increase.[6]

[5](See Kiefer, 2001, p. 294).

[6](See Kiefer, 2001, pp. 295–306).

In Europe, a crucial legal impact is expected from the new motor vehicle block exemptions, introduced explicitly to reduce customer prices.[7] These contain a set of rules which aim at increasing competition by allowing for stand-alone and independent repair shops, multi-brand dealerships, and greater variety of spare parts as well as at facilitating cross country sales. Among other things, the new set of rules may result in independent dealers trying to exploit their position against the manufacturers.

All these trends indicate that competition should further increase in the future, implying that sales considerations are becoming more important. As outlined in section 2.3.1, this may be in conflict with risk management concerns.

3.1.2 Credit Portfolios in the Automotive Industry

Credit exposures at a large captive such as DaimlerChrysler Services, VW Financial Services or GMAC usually range from 12 to 82 months, depending on the business line. The portfolios consist of a large number of corporate and private exposures. As an example, according to the DC Bank annual reports, the portfolio had a volume of EUR 4.797 bn in 2002, increasing from EUR 4.597 bn in 2001. The number of vehicles units in the portfolio increased by 11.5 % to 288,457. These numbers serve as an example for the success of automotive captives at obtaining finance and lease contracts. In turn, it implies the need to manage portfolios of significant sizes.

Regarding the customers, among the corporate exposures few listed companies can be found . Examples for this observation are medium-sized companies with significant exposures in the car fleet management unit, such as logistics companies. For these, stock quotes or detailed accounting information might not be available. Lack of this and other credit relevant information can also be expected for the retail portfolios.

With respect to the riskiness of the behavior, there is anecdotal evidence at least for Germany that car payments are among the last commitments private customers default on. This observation, however, might not be correct in the case of leasing contracts nor relate to corpo-

[7]For the motor vehicle block exemption see http://europa.eu.int/comm/competition/ car_sector.

rate customers. Regarding the exposure, there is usually no volatility since option-like assets are not offered, and credit lines are not available. On the other hand, loss rates are crucial due to the influence of the vehicle collateral. Residual values are expected to be volatile, which has to be considered in the modeling of loss rates. Their influence is also reflected by the internal processes at both the financial service company and the manufacturer itself. These strive to optimize not only the residual value forecast but also the collection and remarketing processes.

3.1.3 Data Availability, Empirical and Modeling Requirements

The choice of a credit risk model must consider data availability. There is currently a lack of credit risk-relevant data in car finance, reflecting the situation in the banking industry. However, the data situation differs between captives. In the context of this thesis, the author has had access to a large quantity of high quality data. These include both internal data, e.g. contract information and residual values, and external data, e.g. industry default rates provided by the Statistisches Bundesamt. Further residual value information from external sources is available, see ABN Amro (2002) or Schmit (2002), but these data cannot be used since only internal data reflect segment-specific losses without statistical distortions due to data pooling.

On the other hand, both economic and statistical analysis is in practice almost always restricted by data shortcomings. In the case of loss rates, more detailed information beyond the residual value is desirable. Residual value and vehicle information is usually restricted to the original vehicle price and the remarketing value. Additional disposal information is difficult to obtain. An example is vehicle condition, which can be expected to influence used car values. This factor should therefore be controlled in loss rate estimation, for example as supplementary segmentation criterion. One reason for the non-availability of such information is that used cars are oftentimes sold in packages, where single car specifications are not tracked.

Finally, customer information is scarce, in particular in the case of retail portfolios. Stock quotes and other market information as well as detailed insights into the balance sheet are however important inputs in some credit risk models. They are, among other things, required to derive default dependencies, which are crucial in all credit risk models.

Regarding the empirical and modeling requirements placed on the credit risk model, volatile and dependent default probabilities must be available in the model. The same is the case for individual remarketing values and thus for loss rates. For portfolio management, the model must allow advanced portfolio risk measures such as the Value at Risk to be calculated. Based on such a measure, it should allow the derivation of individual risk contributions. In spite of the large portfolios to be managed in the automotive industry, the model should also be relatively fast.

3.2 Elements of Credit Risk Modeling

The Basle Committee on Banking Supervision has suggested the following broad definition of credit risk models, which also includes organizational issues. The credit loss of a portfolio can be defined as the difference between its current and future value due to credit risk.

Definition 2 (Credit risk model) *Broadly defined, a credit risk model encompasses all of the policies, procedures and practises used by a bank in estimating a credit portfolio's probability density function [of credit losses].*[8]

With regard to quantitative modeling, figure 3.1 describes the relationships between the key inputs and modeling assumptions. The purpose of a credit risk model is to derive the loss distribution. Based on the loss distribution, loss measures such as the Value at Risk can be calculated in the subsequent step.[9] For the loss distribution, a valuation function, which allows a value to to be assigned to the assets in the portfolio for each realization of the stochastic risk factors, must be constructed. These factors can represent both credit and market risks, with the focus in credit risk lying on the factors probability of default ("PD"), exposure at default ("EAD") and loss given default ("LGD"). These describe the probability that a counterparty will default, the outstanding sum at that time, and the percentage of the outstanding sum that is finally lost. PD and LGD are usually assumed to be percentages, although it can be argued that

[8](See BIS, 1999b, p. 14).

[9]In credit risk, usually relatively high quantiles are used as opposed to market risk, see BIS (1999b), p. 27.

LGDs can be negative. This might be the case with defaulted, overcollateralized loans. In the figure, the PD is generalized in terms of the default class. In loan and lease contracts, customer default is certainly the only relevant credit risk event. But with respect to bond portfolios, for example, the migration risk of up- or downgrading also has an economic impact.[10]

The most important part of credit risk modeling is to determine the multivariate distribution of these risk factors, for each single exposure and across the whole portfolio. This step necessitates modeling both the single distribution of the factors and their dependency structure. The choice of a special approach is contingent on both empirical and practical considerations. Conceptional, parameter, and validation issues as suggested by the Basle Committee are described in the next section.[11]

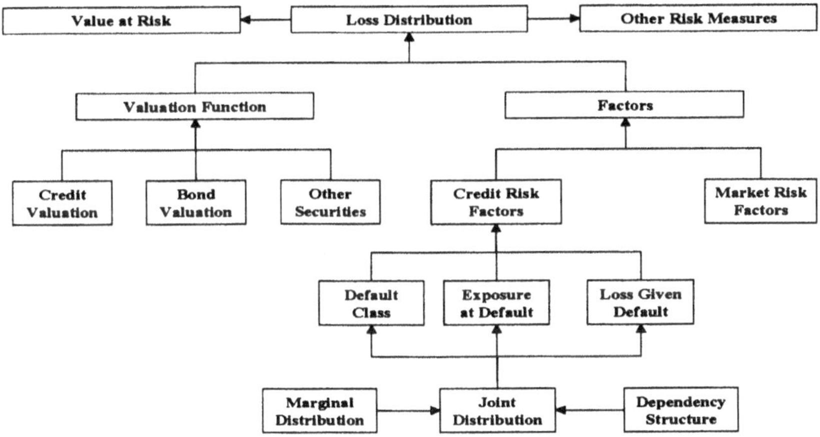

Figure 3.1: The General Structure of Credit Risk Models

[10]See also section 3.2.1.

[11](See BIS, 1999b).

3.2.1 Conceptional Issues

Conceptional issues discussed by the Basle Committee in the context of credit risk models include the definition of credit loss, the time horizon, credit risk aggregation, credit correlations, and the internal application. As suggested in the last section, the credit loss of a portfolio is defined as the difference between its current and the future value due to credit risk. Whereas it is usually not a problem to determine the current value of the portfolio, the latter is ex ante unknown. From this follows that credit loss is stochastic. There are two approaches to evaluating the future value: the mark-to-market ("MTM") and default mode ("DM") models.[12] In MTM models, credit loss can also occur due to credit quality changes without the counterparty actually defaulting. An intuitive example of migration risk is the value of a bond, which is tied to its rating. The DM paradigm is a special case and can be used if credit losses only occur in case of the counterparty's default.

With regard to the time horizon and credit risk aggregation, a consensus born out of necessity and the need for standardization has developed. Generally regarding the time horizon of a credit risk model it is possible to choose between the individual hold-to-maturity or a common interval across all exposures.[13] For three reasons, a uniform time interval of one year is usually employed. First, one year is a common time frame in many other regards such as accounting, so processes need not be adjusted. Second, one year is also the interval chosen by the regulator to calculate credit risk capital requirements. Finally, one year is a compromise between the benefits of a long and a short interval. Yet, there are also arguments against this particular interval. First, a longer time interval can be more representative of a buy-and-hold portfolio. In addition, it may allow to the effects of credit cycles to be better included.

Concerning credit risk aggregation, it has widely been agreed upon that corporate and capital market instruments and consumer, credit card or retail portfolios should be distinguished between. For the former, individual characteristics are usually tracked and processed ("bottom-up"), whereas, for the latter, data are pooled and thus standardized ("top-down").[14] While the

[12](See BIS, 1999b, p. 17).

[13](See BIS, 1999b, p. 16 and p. 24).

[14](See BIS, 1999b, p. 26).

pooling of data facilitates processes, it may on the other hand possibly hide credit specifics.

It seems reasonable to assume that in credit risk models in comparison to market risk models, correlation or more general dependence should play the preeminent role. This is due primarily to the longer time horizon of credit risk models, where relationships are not swamped in the short interval. Also, empirical experience shows that credit risk events such as defaults commonly depend on each other.

Correlations or dependencies between risk parameters can be observed on both the contract level as well as between the different contracts in the portfolio. On the level of the individual contracts, an intuitive example is the question of whether credit lines are drawn when the credit quality of the contract counterparty decreases. In the context of a credit risk model, this would be equivalent to assuming a positive relationship between the PD and the EAD. However, as the Basle Committee put it in 1999, "although banks tend to be aware of ... [such] potential relationships, their ability to model such correlations is often limited in practice".[15] The most important example of parameter dependencies across the portfolio are, of course, dependencies between the individual PD parameters.

3.2.2 Parameter Specification

In general, the assumptions about the distribution of risk factors are a key element in the design of credit risk models.[16] But although the specification and estimation of the input parameters might seem of less importance from a modeling perspective, in practice the quality of the results of credit risk models might be distorted much more by badly estimated parameters than by the conceptional model.[17] The relative importance of modeling is also reflected by the empirical and theoretical finding that popular models produce similar results given appropriately adjusted inputs.[18]

The specification and estimation of risk parameters is important, but multiple problems ex-

[15](See BIS, 1999b, p. 31).

[16](See for example Hirtle et al., 2001, p. 21).

[17](See BIS, 1999b, p. 35).

[18](See for example Bröker and Lehrbass, 2001, p. 779).

ist in practice beyond data availability. First, the risk parameters relate to different spheres, since both LGD and EAD are transaction specific, whereas the PD is specific of the counterparty. The merging of the two spheres is not only difficult with regard to the internal IT systems. In addition, the dependency structure between the parameters should be taken into account for estimation purposes, if not for modeling. This is, however, not always feasible. Empirical and theoretical results regarding the dependencies are also not homogeneous. For example, Bröker and Lehrbass (2001), p. 778, find general indications that the interdependencies between the three risk parameters are weak. For the relationships between loss and default rates, Society of Actuaries (1998) and Asarnow and Edwards (1995) find the same results. On the other hand, a study conducted by Moody's Investor Service indicates that recovery rates are correlated with the economic cycle.[19] From this follows that at least implied dependencies between loss and default rates should exist. The survey described in Allen and Saunders (2002) confirms this opposite view and thus the overall inconclusive picture.

Instead, most models employ simplifying assumptions such as independent, deterministic risk factors or identical distributions within segments. The implications of these assumptions regarding both modeling and estimation of the risk factors are not yet fully understood.[20]

3.2.3 Backtesting and Alternatives for Validation

> *While this section [on credit risk modeling] raises many conceptual issues regarding the various approaches, the question of the materiality of each is an empirical one.*
>
> BIS (1999b), p. 13

> *The results indicate that, unless a relatively long performance history or historical simulation data base is available, there are significant statistical difficulties surrounding verification of VaR estimates.*
>
> Kupiec (1995), p. 74

[19](See Moody's Investors Service, 2000).

[20](See BIS, 1999b, p. 5).

We can't define it [Stress Tests], but we know it when we see it.

Supreme Court Justice Potter Stewart, cited in Berkowitz (2000)

The three quotes above well summarize the current situation faced in the statistical validation, or backtesting, of credit risk models. As a result of the general data scarcity and the long forecast horizon of credit risk models, it seems unlikely that a purely quantitative validation of credit risk models will be available in the near future.[21] As a substitute or addition to backtesting, stress testing has been suggested also by regulators.[22] Stress testing is based on a subjective scenario analysis where the model results are calculated for extreme realizations of the input factors.[23] The choice of a stress test scenario is by its very nature subjective. This makes the external review of a bank's stress testing program, for example by regulators, extremely difficult.[24]

Extensive research is available on backtesting, whereas literature on stress testing is scarce most likely due to the subjective components involved. For this reason, Lopez (2000) argues that standardized approaches rightly do not exist, although scenarios should be internally consistent.[25] A general procedure is given in Berkowitz (2000), p. 4, where four types of shocks are differentiated which can be utilized in the scenarios . First and second, these are events that either have been very rare historically, or which have never occurred. Third, scenarios can involve shocks to the statistical patterns of a model such as the dependency structure. Finally, shocks can occur when structural breaks occur, e.g. judicial changes in bankruptcy law.

3.2.4 Implications for the Automotive Industry

The specific situation in the automotive industry has implications for the issues outlined in the foregoing. Regarding the definition of credit loss, a default mode model is sufficient for the buy-and-hold loan portfolios under consideration. With respect to the time horizon, to ensure

---

[21](See for example Hirtle et al., 2001, p. 29).

[22](See for example BIS, 1999b).

[23](See Lopez, 2000).

[24](See Berkowitz, 2000, p. 3).

[25]The approach of Kupiec (1998) focuses exclusively on the CreditMetrics framework.

the comparability of economic to regulatory capital requirements and in accordance with industry practice an interval of one year is chosen. Concerning dependencies, both default and loss rate correlations are modeled, but no correlations between default and loss rates. Neglecting exposure volatility can be justified by the observation that, in car finance and lease contracts, credit lines and payment structures are fixed. With respect to further hypotheses concerning, for example, the relationship between PD and the LGD, there is not sufficient conclusive empirical evidence.

The approach for choosing a credit risk model supported in this thesis is the use of assumptions based on historical and anecdotal observations. Under this approach, modelers must be aware of and clearly separate quantitative and qualitative building blocks. The validation of the overall model is then restricted to the modular validation of these assumptions. The parameter estimation process is described in detail in chapter 7 which sets out the empirical study.

3.3 Model Selection

3.3.1 Short History of Credit Risk Models

Historically, 1997 was a crucial year for credit risk modeling. Three models were published that year which are still of importance today. First, JP Morgan developed a reduced-form approach called CreditMetrics. CreditMetrics is in extensive use today and serves as an industry benchmark, although it is often criticized for its limited applicability to loan portfolios. Later that year, Credit Suisse First Boston published CreditRisk+ ("CR+"), which had been inspired by actuarial models. CR+ offers the particular feature of an analytical solution without the need for Monte Carlo simulation. Finally, the management consultancy McKinsey published CreditPortfolioView, an econometric model ascribing default rate volatility to macroeconomic factors. These publications may have been motivated by the creators' attempt to ensure future consulting fees, but the models also showed both the industry and the regulators that quantitative credit risk modeling is possible. They served to standardize terms and notions and promoted the move from a buy-and-hold policy towards active credit risk management.

The evolution of credit risk models and models for credit-linked derivatives has gone forward since then. New models strive to overcome weaknesses of old models, or to exploit new economic and mathematical results, such as Credit Suisse First Boston's unpublished PortfolioRisk+. PortfolioRisk+ is not commercially available but is only provided to CSFB's customers.[26] It is based on saddlepoint approximations of quantiles of the loss distribution, which avoid simulation and provide a convenient way to estimate Value at Risk and risk contributions. A key focus of current research is the merger of credit with market risk models, such a model is for example developed in Reiß (2003).[27] A recent survey of credit risk models can be found in the fourth chapter of Allen et al. (2004). On the other hand, the increasing complexity of credit risk models can countermeasure their flexibility and scalability, i.e. the applicability of a model to heterogeneous portfolios of varying size.[28] For just these reasons, in reaction to inquiries on credit risk management by the Basle Committee, it was mentioned that usage of a single model for the whole portfolio would be disadvantageous. Instead, different models which are suitable for different types of portfolios, such as loan and bond portfolios, should be employed.[29]

3.3.2 Classification of Credit Risk Models

Different classifications of credit risk models have been proposed. A popular example is given in Crouhy et al. (2000) and Jackson et al. (1999), where four different classes are differentiated along which most models can be aligned. First, models can be based on the option framework for credit risk as developed by Merton in 1974. Such models are frequently referred to as option-type or structural models. For this class, a simplified model of the firm's capital structure is assumed. A firm is considered to be in default when the total value of its assets falls below that of its liabilities. In this case the owners would execute an implicit put option to sell the firm.[30] The most popular representative of this class is the model developed by the KMV corporation, which for implementation purposes makes extensive use of KMV's historical data

[26]See Risk, March 1994, "PortfolioRisk+ cracks the tail conundrum".

[27](See also Crouhy et al., 2000, p. 61).

[28](See Bröker and Lehrbass, 2001, p. 779).

[29]For a summary of the responses see http://www.bis.org/publ/bcbs71.htm#ptop.

[30](See Crouhy et al., 2000).

base to derive default probabilities based on company information. Correlations are derived from indices representing common factors.

The second group of credit risk models is rating based, a popular example being CreditMetrics. The latter models a latent variable indicating default and utilizes indices to derive dependencies between defaults. In contrast to option-models, rating migrations including default are based on historical transition matrices.[31] Employing a normal distribution, different intervals under the distribution function are then assigned to correspond to the different potential ratings by fitting the discrete transition probabilities from the transition matrix. The discrete distribution generated this way is then utilized for Monte Carlo simulations.[32]

The third group of models are based on macroeconomic considerations. The most widely used among these is CreditPortfolioView. This class of models hinge on the observation that default probabilities are related to the macroeconomic climate. Thus, factors such as the gross domestic product, interest rate levels, and exchange or saving rates are used in a regression type model. Dependencies between defaults are modeled and estimated by dependencies between the macroeconomic factors. The estimated parameters are then employed to simulate the loss distribution. In contrast to the first two classes of models, macroeconomic models are typically default models and do not model rating migrations.[33]

Finally, actuarial models are based on concepts derived in insurance models. Such models use the analogy between customer defaults and insurance events, but do not consider migration or spread risk. The most popular model in this class is CreditRisk+ ("CR+"). In CR+, the default event is only indirectly modeled by introducing default rate volatility via random PDs. A higher realized PD, then, corresponds to an increased likelihood of default. The random PDs are modeled as transformations of stochastic sector default rates. If PDs are based on one or more common sector default rate, dependencies between defaults are introduced.[34] In contrast to the three other classes, actuarial models provide a closed solution without the need

[31]Transition matrices describe for each possible pair of credit states the probability of the change from one into the other.

[32]For more information see http://www.riskmetrics.com.

[33]For more information see Wilson (1997a) and Wilson (1997b).

[34]For more information see section 4.1.

for Monte Carlo simulation. Although processing time requirements are constantly decreasing, simulations are still time consuming and may distort results.[35]

3.3.3 Comparability and Mixtures of Models

There are remarkable parallels between different models, with respect to both the underlying theory and the results as shown by Koyluoglu and Hickman (1998) or Finger (1998), for example. In particular, the two well-known models CR+ and CreditMetrics can be translated into each other.[36] Regarding results, a joint study of credit risk models by the International Swaps and Derivatives Association ISDA and the Institute of International Finance IIF came to the conclusion that "models yield directionally consistent outputs when given similar inputs".[37] The study was built on portfolios provided by 25 commercial banks from 10 countries with varying sizes and specialties. Implemented were four publicly available models: CreditMetrics, CreditPortfolioView, PortfolioManager and CR+. It also concluded that "no two banks are likely to implement a credit risk model in an identical manner".[38] Similar results at least for well-diversified portfolios are provided in Jackson et al. (1999). The study examined the Eurobond market using the two credit risk models KMV and CreditMetrics. These results indicate the importance of the correct calculation of risk parameters such as PD, LGD or the dependency estimators in comparison to the correct model choice. Christoffersen et al. (2001), pp. 1-2, employ the term "implementation risk", as opposed to "model risk", to describe this phenomenon.

For a variety of other reasons practitioners tend to be skeptical as to whether an generally best model exists. The first reason is that given the present state of experience and scarce data availability, correct backtesting of the model as a whole will not be possible for the near future.[39] [40] In practice, at least one of the following data requirements usually is not confirmed

[35]For some practical problems see Cifuentes and O'Connor (1996), p. 1.

[36](See Gordy, 2000).

[37](See Institute of International Finance, 2000, p. 2).

[38](See Institute of International Finance, 2000, p. 3).

[39](See for example Bröker and Lehrbass, 2001, p. 779).

[40]Lopez (2000) suggests a resampling approach to avoid data restrictions. These approach is however statisti-

to. First, the data history should be comprehensive, covering the full credit cycle. Second, the data should be bank specific and finally be based on standardized definitions especially regarding the default event.[41] Another reason against the assumption of a single best model is the heterogeneous environment in which credit risk models are used. This has led in practice to the application of different models to different portfolios at the same institution.

Yet, this does not moot the need for internal quantitative credit risk models. As Alan Greenspanof the US federal reserve noted, "formal risk management models are essential in providing a consistent analytic framework for collecting, organizing and summarizing information about individual risk exposures so that bank managers ... can assess the institution's overall risk profile in a rational and comprehensive manner".[42]

3.3.4 Applicability of Model Types to Auto Portfolios

As noted in subsection 3.2.4, the consideration of default mode models is sufficient in the case of auto portfolios. Thus, none of the four model types can be ruled out. With regard to the empirical requirements, especially the modeling of loss rate volatility is of importance. Basically, due to the vehicle collateral, car finance and lease contracts have small LGDs. They might, however, be very volatile. This feature can be modeled in all four types of models.

On the other hand, the application of option-type and ratings-based models is not feasible for two reasons. First, stock quotations are not available for significant parts of the portfolios, e.g. retail or small and medium companies. With special regard to option-type models, detailed balance sheet information is oftentimes missing, proscribing the proper modeling of assets and liabilities. Regarding the general applicability of macroeconomic models, they require that contracts or customers be linked to segments for which significant data, e.g. default rates, are available. This information is, however, currently not available- at least for the retail portfolio. Thus, only actuarial models allow a unifying approach across the overall portfolio.

---

cally fallible.

[41](See Hirtle et al., 2001, p. 28).

[42]For the complete speech, see http://www.federalreserve.com/boarddocs/speeches/2002/ 200020510/default.htm.

This conclusion does not imply that there are not model types which may be suited better for isolated subportfolios. If different models were to be implemented together, actuarial models could be employed for retail portfolios and, for example, option-type models for corporate customers. Neglecting the availability of customer information however, such a mixed model approach must be rejected in the context of this thesis. Given the requirement of individual risk contributions, Monte Carlo simulations for large portfolios are not feasible since they are too time consuming.[43] This again rules out the three types of models which use simulations: the option-type, rating-based and macro-economic models. Another general problem that occurs when different models are simultaneously applied to different subportfolios is how to combine the information given by the individual loss distributions or risk measures.

Thus, in the specific context of this thesis, actuarial models must be used exclusively. The most popular actuarial model is CR+, which is implemented in this thesis. CR+ meets all the requirements pointed out; among other attributes it is parsimonious, offers a fast algorithm for both the loss distribution and individual risk contributions, and thanks to extensions of the original model offers the possibility to include loss rate volatility. Also, although published in 1997, CR+ is still the object of extensive research. In the next section, examples of implementations of CR+ at different institutions are described.

3.3.5 Implementations of CR+

Although the implementation of a credit risk model is more an applied than a theoretical issue, there have been a number of publications targeting this issue. Bolder et al. (2002) describe an application of CR+ for portfolios of mortgage loans, focusing on loss rate volatility. Using the model of Bürgisser et al. (2001) for a simulated portfolio, the authors conclude that loss rate volatility has a significant effect on the quantiles of the loss distribution. In this paper the framework developed in Lehrbass (2000) is employed, in which CR+ is employed to calculate fair rates for tranches of mortgage loan securitizations. In comparison to this thesis, these researchers neglect individual risk contributions and the choice of contracts for securitization,

[43] A general critical discussion of simulation as a tool is given, for example, in Jorion (2001), pp. 299.

while analyzing the subsequent question of how to price ABS tranches.

Schmit (2002) implements a modified version of CR+ for an empirical analysis of automotive lease contracts. His adaption of the original model is motivated by the negligence of loss rate volatility in the original model and employs Monte Carlo simulation. By comparison, in this thesis the CR+ version of Bürgisser et al. (2001) is used to incorporate stochastic loss rates without the need for simulation. Of particular interest to practitioners should be the implementation of the basic CR+ model at Westdeutsche Landesbank Girozentrale ("WestLB") set out in Bröker and Lehrbass (2001). At this institution, CR+ has been in use for integrated risk reporting and analysis since 1998.

Chapter 4

CreditRisk+ and the Regulatory Model

4.1 The Original CreditRisk+ Model

4.1.1 Introduction and Survey

The original version of CreditRisk+ ("CR+") is a default model for the loss distribution of a credit portfolio.[1] Thus, it models portfolio losses due to borrower defaults only, but not due to migration risk. It is based on concepts from insurance mathematics, and uses the parallel between default and insurance events. Dependencies between defaults are modeled implicitly by conditioning individual default probabilities on common, independent sector default rates. If the latter are high, individual default rates are also high, implying dependencies between defaults. Conditionally, default events are independent. A simpler version without default rate volatility and thus without dependencies has also been suggested. Loss rates are originally deterministic, which allows them to be absorbed into the net exposure. To obtain a discrete loss variable for analytical ease, these net exposures are standardized and rounded. Under these assumptions, CR+ provides an analytical solution for the loss distribution without the need for Monte Carlo simulations.

It is also important to analyze what is not modeled in the original CR+ model: CR+ does not model rating migration and exposure volatility. This is, however, not of relevance for

[1]The following discussion is motivated by Lehrbass et al. (2001) and Wilde (1997a).

large parts of automotive portfolios. Moreover, extensions of the original CR+ model which allow for rating migrations exist.[2] A further point is the lack of single default event modeling. Instead, the loss distribution is calculated for the overall portfolio, and risk contributions hinge exclusively on the aggregate risk measures based on it. Significant individual exposure in particular should for this reason also be monitored separately.

4.1.2 Data Requirements

Data requirements for CR+ are few and vary slightly between models. For all models, a standardization unit L must be set. In the original model without default rate volatility, each contract $i \in I$ in the portfolio is assigned a probability of default ("PD") PD_i and a deterministic (net) exposure equivalent to $LGD_i EAD_i$. In the original model with default rate volatility, additionally the PD volatility and sector weights assigning borrowers to sector default rates are required.

Bürgisser et al. (1999) suggest a model with dependent sector default rates. This modification of the original model also requires sector default rate correlations. An improvement of the latter model allows for both dependent sector default rates and loss rate volatility.[3] For implementation, individual net exposures must be split into a deterministic exposure and stochastic loss rates. In addition to the exposure, the average individual loss rate and its volatility as well as correlations between loss rate sectors must be provided.

Wehrspohn (2002) discusses in detail problems arising from usage of proxies for input calculation. This implies a shift from model to parameterization risk. In the automotive industry, this concerns loss rates in particular, which are significantly influenced by vehicle collateral.

4.2 Framework of CreditRisk+

In this section, the formal model is introduced, focusing on the description of the underlying assumptions. First, probability generating functions which are used extensively in the CR+

[2](See Rolfes and Broeker, 1998).

[3](See Bürgisser et al., 2001).

model are introduced. Subsequently, the model is developed stepwise.

4.2.1 Probability Generating Functions

Probability generating functions ("PGF") provide a convenient way to calculate especially discrete probabilities for aggregations of random variables. For a discrete random variable X, the PGF is given by:

$$F_X(z) = E\left(z^X\right) = \sum z^x P(X = x)$$

Some important results relate to moments and aggregations of random variables via the PGF.[4] In the following, let X and X_i denote independent and discrete random variables and $F_X(z)$ the PGF of X.

1. The expected value and the variance of X can be formulated as:

$$\begin{aligned} E(X) &= F'_X(1) \\ V(X) &= F''_X(1) + F'_X(1) - F'_X(1)^2 \end{aligned}$$

2. The probability distribution of X can be calculated as:

$$\begin{aligned} P(X = 0) &= F_X(0) \\ P(X = x \neq 0) &= \left.\frac{d^x}{(dz)^x} F_X(z)\right|_{z=0} \end{aligned}$$

3. The PGF of a sum of independent random variables is equal to the product of the individual PGFs:

$$F_{\sum_i X_i}(z) = \prod_i F_{X_i}(z)$$

4. The unconditional can be computed from the conditional PGF by integrating out the conditioning variable:

$$F_{X_i}(z) = \sum_y F_{X_i|X_j=y}(z) P(X_j = y)$$

[4](See for example Gordy, 2000, p. 122).

4.2.2 Assumption I : Default independence conditional on individual default rates

Defaults in CR+ are modeled as Bernoulli experiments, where it is assumed that the defaults are independent when conditioned on the risk drivers. Bernoulli random variables have one parameter that describes the probability that an event will occur. This translates to the default probability of a borrower i in the context of a credit risk. If the default probability $\widetilde{X}_i$ is stochastic, this random variable is called the default rate. By construction, the assigned probabilities of default PD_i are equal to the mean default rates. The CR+ methodology includes models both for deterministic default rates, where the default rate is set equal to PD_i, and for stochastic default rates.

For Bernoulli experiments, the derivation of the PGF is straightforward. Regardless of whether dealing with a fixed or stochastic default rate, conditionally on the realization p_i of the default rate $\widetilde{X}_i$, the PGF $F_i(z)$ of the default of borrower i can be computed as:[5]

$$F_i(z|p_i) = E\left(z^I\right) = p_i * z^1 + (1 - p_i) * z^0 = 1 + p_i(z - 1)$$

Thus, the PGF of the total number of defaults, computed as product of the individual PGFs due to the conditional independence given p_i, is:

$$F(z|p_1, ..., p_n) = \prod_{i \in I} F_i(z) = \prod_{i \in I} \left[1 + p_{i(z-1)}\right]$$

4.2.3 Assumption II : Approximation of probability generating function

Given small realized default rates p_i, the PGF of both individual default and the total number of defaults can be approximated by the PGF of a Poisson distribution. This can be demonstrated two ways. First, the linear approximation for small y $\ln(1 + y) \approx y$ can be used to show that the individual PGFs $F_i(z|p_i)$ can be approximated by:

$$F_i(z|p_i) = e^{\ln(1+p_i(z-1))} \approx e^{p_i(z-1)}$$

[5](See Wilde, 1997a, p. 34).

Alternatively, $F_i(z|p_i)$ can be treated as an approximation of the exponential polynomial that neglects higher order terms:[6]

$$e^{p_i(z-1)} = 1 + \frac{p_i\,(z-1)}{1!} + \frac{[p_i\,(z-1)]^2}{2!} + \ldots \approx 1 + p_i\,(z-1) = F_i(z|p_i)$$

The approximation is of the same form as the PGF of a Poisson distributed random variable X with parameter λ, which can be calculated as:

$$E\left[z^X\right] = \sum_{i=0}^{\infty} z^i \frac{\lambda^i}{i!} e^{-\lambda} = e^{\lambda(z-1)}$$

For the approximation to be valid, small p_i equivalent to the λ of the Poisson distribution are required. These ensure that no borrower defaults more than once.

The approximated PGF of the total number of defaults $F(z|p_1, ..., p_n)$ also takes the form of a Poisson PGF:[7]

$$F\,(z|p_1, ..., p_n) = e^{\sum_{i\in I} p_i(z-1)} = e^{\mu(z-1)}$$

where :

$$\mu = \sum_{i\in I} p_i$$

4.2.4 Assumption III : Functional form of the individual default rates

If default rates are assumed to be stochastic, the underlying risk drivers in the basic model are exclusively sector-specific scaling factors $\widetilde{X}^{(s)}$, which can be interpreted as sector default rates.[8] From these, the stochastic default rates $\widetilde{X}_i$ are derived as a weighted sum. The sector weights $\theta_i^{(s)}$ of borrower i depend on the amount of risk with respect to the individual default rate of borrower i that is assigned to sector s. For all borrowers, the sum of the sector weights is equal to one, and the following functional form is assumed for the individual default rates:[9]

$$\widetilde{X}_i = PD_i \cdot \sum_{s\in S} \theta_i^{(s)} \cdot \widetilde{X}^{(s)}$$

[6] (See Lehrbass et al., 2001, p. 11).

[7] (See Wilde, 1997a, p. 34).

[8] The interpretation of sector default rates is discussed in more detail in section 4.4.2.

[9] In accordance with Lehrbass et al. (2001), p. 19, without loss of generality it is assumed that $E(\widetilde{X}^{(s)}) = 1$.

From this follows for μ:

$$\mu = \sum_{i \in I} \left(PD_i \cdot \sum_{s \in S} \theta_i^{(s)} \cdot \widetilde{X}^{(s)} \right) = \sum_{s \in S} \left[\left(\sum_{i \in I} \theta_i^{(s)} \cdot PD_i \right) \cdot \widetilde{X}^{(s)} \right]$$

4.2.5 Idiosyncratic Sectors

As opposed to diversifiable risk, which decreases in portfolio size and granularity, idiosyncratic risk is asset specific and cannot be diversified away. In addition to this intuitive motivation for modeling, idiosyncratic risk is of practical interest in applications for retail portfolios. For these, correlations are difficult to estimate, and idiosyncratic risk can serve as a substitute risk driver. To model idiosyncratic risk in CR+, one solution is to include individual sectors for single or for each contract in the portfolio.[10] These can be either volatile, or degenerate with variance zero and uniformly set equal to one. If one idiosyncratic sector with index 0 is used, this implies that $\widetilde{X}^{(0)} = 1$. If the weights of this sector are denoted by $\theta_i^{(0)}$, the following form of individual default rates $\widetilde{X}_i'$ and of μ' is obtained:

$$\begin{aligned}
\widetilde{X}_i' &= PD_i \cdot \left(\theta_i^{(0)} + \sum_{s \in S} \theta_i^{(s)} \cdot \widetilde{X}^{(s)} \right) \Rightarrow \\
\mu' &= \sum_{i \in I} \left(PD_i \cdot \left(\theta_i^{(0)} + \sum_{s \in S} \theta_i^{(s)} \cdot \widetilde{X}^{(s)} \right) \right) \\
&= \sum_{i \in I} PD_i \cdot \theta_i^{(0)} + \sum_{s \in S} \left[\left(\sum_{i \in I} \theta_i^{(s)} \cdot PD_i \right) \cdot \widetilde{X}^{(s)} \right]
\end{aligned}$$

4.2.6 Assumption IV : Independent gamma distributions of sector default rates

Given the PGF of the conditional number of defaults, the unconditional PGF of defaults can be derived by "integrating out" the conditioning random variables, i.e. the sector default rates. For analytical ease, these are assumed to be independent and gamma distributed. The unconditional PGF can thus be computed as:

$$F(z) = \int \cdots \int \exp\left(\mu (z-1)\right) \cdot f\left(\widetilde{X}^{(1)}, ..., \widetilde{X}^{(S)}\right) \cdot dx^{(1)} \cdot \ldots \cdot dx^{(S)}$$

[10] See Wilde (1997a), § A12.3, or Gordy (2001a), p. 3.

Due to the independence of the sectors, the multivariate density $f\left(\widetilde{X}^{(1)},...,\widetilde{X}^{(S)}\right)$ is equal to the product of the marginals, and the integrals can be computed separately. Plugging in the formula for μ and the gamma density with parameters $\alpha^{(s)}$ and $\beta^{(s)}$ for $f\left(\widetilde{X}^{(s)}\right)$, $F(z)$ can be expressed as product over all sectors of integrals $A^{(s)}$ defined as:

$$A^{(s)} = \int \exp\left(\left(\sum_{i\in I}\theta_i^{(s)}\cdot PD_i\right)\cdot x\cdot(z-1)\right)\cdot\frac{x^{\alpha^{(s)}-1}\cdot\exp\left(-\frac{x}{\beta^{(s)}}\right)}{\left(\beta^{(s)}\right)^{\alpha^{(s)}}\cdot\Gamma\left(\alpha^{(s)}\right)}\cdot dx \qquad (4.1)$$

Part of the integral can be transformed into a Gamma function, which is why the Poisson approximation is of such great importance.[11] Canceling leaves:

$$\begin{aligned} A^{(s)} &= \left(\frac{1}{1-z\cdot\mu^{(s)}\cdot\beta^{(s)}+\mu^{(s)}\cdot\beta^{(s)}}\right)^{\alpha} \\ &= \left(\frac{1-\delta^{(s)}}{1-\delta^{(s)}\cdot z}\right)^{\alpha^{(s)}} \end{aligned}$$

where $\delta = \frac{\mu^{(s)}\cdot\beta^{(s)}}{1+\mu^{(s)}\cdot\beta^{(s)}}$ and $\mu^{(s)} = \sum_{i\in I}\theta_i^{(s)}\cdot PD_i$.[12]

If the other integrals are solved analogously, the unconditional PGF of the total number of losses is given by:

$$F(z) = \prod_{s\in S}\left(\frac{1-\delta^{(s)}}{1-\delta^{(s)}\cdot z}\right)^{\alpha^{(s)}}$$

Inclusion of the idiosyncratic sector yields a PGF of the following form:

$$F'(z) = \exp\left(\left[\sum_{i\in I}PD_i\cdot\theta_i^{(0)}\right]\cdot(z-1)\right)\cdot\prod_{s\in S}\left(\frac{1-\delta^{(s)}}{1-\delta^{(s)}\cdot z}\right)^{\alpha^{(s)}}$$

4.2.7 Assumption V : Rounding and standardizing of exposures

Losses are induced exclusively by defaults, since credit spreads due to rating migrations are not modeled. Thus, for a borrower with exposure LGD_iEAD_i, the probability of a loss of LGD_iEAD_i can be set equal to the probability of defaulting.[13] To derive the PGF of losses in

[11] Exact calculations are in the appendix.

[12] This form is equivalent to the PGF of a random variable with negative binomial distribution.

[13] In the original version as outlined in Wilde (1997a), loss rates are deterministic. The extension to stochastic loss rates is described in section 4.3.2.

analogy to the derivation of defaults, it is necessary to discretize losses by rounding. To additionally reduce the number of computations for the total loss distribution, it is also suggested that the exposures be standardized by dividing them by a standard unit L: $\nu_i = L_i \ /L$. Then, they are aligned into discrete bands $m \in M$, where each contract that belongs to a band is assumed to have an identical exposure ν_m. Band m is defined as follows:[14]

$$\text{Band m} = \{i \in I | \nu_i \in (\nu_{m-1}, \nu_m]\}$$

4.2.8 Computation of the Unconditional Loss Distribution

If $G_i(z|p_i)$ denotes the conditional PGF of individual losses, it can be seen that $G_i(z|p_i) = F_i(z^{\nu_i}|p_i)$ from:

$$\begin{aligned} F_i(z|p_i) &= P\left(\tilde{I}_i = 0\right) * z^0 + P\left(\tilde{I}_i = 1\right) * z^1 \\ G_i(z|p_i) &= P\left(\tilde{L}_i = 0\right) * z^0 + P\left(\tilde{L}_i = \nu_i\right) * z^{\nu_i} \end{aligned}$$

Here $\tilde{L}_i$ denotes the loss from borrower i, and $\tilde{I}_i$ is the default indicator. Since the exposures have been discretized, the total loss PGF $G(z|p_1, ..., p_n)$ can be computed as follows, assuming conditional independence:

$$\begin{aligned} G\left(z|\tilde{X}_1, ..., \tilde{X}_n\right) &= \prod_{i \in I} F_i\left(z^{\nu_i}\left|\tilde{X}_i\right.\right) = \exp\left(\sum_{i \in I} \tilde{X}_i\left(z^{\nu_i} - 1\right)\right) \\ &= \exp\left(\sum_{s \in S}\left[\left(\sum_{i \in I}\theta_i^{(s)} \cdot PD_i \cdot \left(z^{\nu_i} - 1\right)\right) \cdot \tilde{X}^{(s)}\right]\right) \end{aligned}$$

The conditioning factors can be integrated out in analogy to the computation of $F(z)$. If all integrals are solved in analogy to the PGF of the total number of defaults, the unconditional PGF of the total loss is:[15]

$$G(z) = \prod_{s \in S}\left(\frac{1 - \delta^{(s)}}{1 - \frac{\delta^{(s)}}{\mu^{(s)}} \cdot \sum_{i \in I}\theta_i^{(s)} \cdot PD_i \cdot z^{\nu_i}}\right)^{\alpha^{(s)}} \tag{4.2}$$

[14]Rounding the exposures up is a deviation from the original approach described in Wilde (1997a) and is suggested, for example, in Lehrbass et al. (2001). The rounding issue will be further discussed in section 4.4.2.

[15]Exact calculations are given in the appendix.

where $\delta^{(s)} = \frac{\mu^{(s)} \cdot \beta^{(s)}}{1+\mu^{(s)} \cdot \beta^{(s)}}$, $\mu^{(s)} = \sum_{i \in I} \theta_i^{(s)} \cdot PD_i$ and $\alpha^{(s)}$ and $\beta^{(s)}$ are the parameters of the sector default rates.

Should an idiosyncratic sector be used, the following form for the unconditional PGF of total loss $G'(z)$ is obtained:

$$G'(z) = \exp\left(\left[\sum_{i \in I} PD_i \cdot \theta_i^{(0)}\right] \cdot (z^{\nu_i} - 1)\right) \cdot \prod_{s \in S} \left(\frac{1 - \delta^{(s)}}{1 - \frac{\delta^{(s)}}{\mu^{(s)}} \cdot \sum_{i \in I} \theta_i^{(s)} \cdot PD_i \cdot z^{\nu_i}}\right)^{\alpha^{(s)}}$$

4.2.9 Implied Dependency Structure

Dependencies between default events are modeled implicitly in CR+ through the introduction of common sectors. This does not mean that it is impossible to quantify dependency measures such as correlations. In CR+, both the correlations between individual stochastic default rates and between the default events themselves can at least be approximately quantified. This is the content of the following two theorems.[16]

Theorem 1 *The correlation between the individual default rates $\widetilde{X}_i$ and $\widetilde{X}_j$ of two contracts i and j in CR+ is given by:*

$$Cor\left(\widetilde{X}_1, \widetilde{X}_2\right) = \frac{A}{\sqrt{\sum_{s \in S} \left(\theta_1^{(s)}\right)^2 \cdot V\left(\widetilde{X}^{(s)}\right)} \cdot \sqrt{\sum_{s \in S} \left(\theta_2^{(s)}\right)^2 \cdot V\left(\widetilde{X}^{(s)}\right)}}$$

where

$$\begin{aligned} A \ := \ & \sum_{s \in S} \theta_1^{(s)} \cdot \theta_2^{(s)} \cdot \left[\left(\alpha^{(s)} \cdot \beta^{(s)}\right)^2 + \alpha^{(s)} \cdot \left(\beta^{(s)}\right)^2\right] \\ & + \sum_{s \in S} \sum_{t \neq s} \theta_1^{(s)} \cdot \theta_2^{(t)} \cdot \alpha^{(s)} \cdot \beta^{(s)} \cdot \alpha^{(t)} \cdot \beta^{(t)} \end{aligned}$$

Proof. Let $\widetilde{X}_1$ and $\widetilde{X}_2$ denote the individual default rates of two contracts 1 and 2 in the portfolio, where:

$$\widetilde{X}_i = PD_i \cdot \sum_{s \in S} \theta_i^{(s)} \cdot \widetilde{X}^{(s)}$$

[16](See Lehrbass et al., 2001, pp. 24).

Then their correlation is defined as:

$$Cor\left(\widetilde{X}_1, \widetilde{X}_2\right) = \frac{Cov\left(\widetilde{X}_1, \widetilde{X}_2\right)}{\sqrt{V\left(\widetilde{X}_1\right) \cdot V(\widetilde{X}_2)}} = \frac{E\left[\widetilde{X}_1 \cdot \widetilde{X}_2\right] - E\left[\widetilde{X}_1\right] \cdot E\left[\widetilde{X}_2\right]}{\sqrt{V\left(\widetilde{X}_1\right) \cdot V(\widetilde{X}_2)}}$$

It remains to compute $E\left[\widetilde{X}_1 \cdot \widetilde{X}_2\right]$, since $E\left[\widetilde{X}_i\right] = PD_i$ and, due to the independence of the sectors:

$$V\left(\widetilde{X}_i\right) = \sum_{s \in S} \left(PD_i \cdot \theta_i^{(s)}\right)^2 \cdot V\left(\widetilde{X}^{(s)}\right)$$

Plugging in the formula of the individual default rates, and given the independence of the sector gamma distributions, yields the following result:

$$\begin{aligned}
E\left[\widetilde{X}_1 \cdot \widetilde{X}_2\right] &= E\left[\left(PD_1 \cdot \sum_{s \in S} \theta_1^{(s)} \cdot \widetilde{X}^{(s)}\right)\left(PD_2 \cdot \sum_{s \in S} \theta_2^{(s)} \cdot \widetilde{X}^{(s)}\right)\right] \\
&= \sum_{s \in S} PD_1 \cdot \theta_1^{(s)} \cdot PD_2 \cdot \theta_2^{(s)} \cdot E\left[\widetilde{X}^{(s)} \cdot \widetilde{X}^{(s)}\right] \\
&\quad + \sum_{s \in S} \sum_{t \neq s} PD_1 \cdot \theta_1^{(s)} \cdot PD_2 \cdot \theta_2^{(t)} \cdot E\left[\widetilde{X}^{(s)}\right] \cdot E\left[\widetilde{X}^{(t)}\right] \\
&= \sum_{s \in S} PD_1 \cdot \theta_1^{(s)} \cdot PD_2 \cdot \theta_2^{(s)} \cdot \left[\left(\alpha^{(s)} \cdot \beta^{(s)}\right)^2 + \alpha^{(s)} \cdot \left(\beta^{(s)}\right)^2\right] \\
&\quad + \sum_{s \in S} \sum_{t \neq s} PD_1 \cdot \theta_1^{(s)} \cdot PD_2 \cdot \theta_2^{(t)} \cdot \alpha^{(s)} \cdot \beta^{(s)} \cdot \alpha^{(t)} \cdot \beta^{(t)}
\end{aligned}$$

Inserting these into the correlation formula and reducing returns the final result. ■

The correlation of the default indicator variables is also of interest for the evaluation of the model.

Theorem 2 *The correlation between default indicators $\tilde{I}_1$ and $\tilde{I}_2$ representing the defaults of two borrowers* 1 *and* 2 *can be approximated as:*

$$Cor(\tilde{I}_1, \tilde{I}_2) \approx \sqrt{PD_1 \cdot PD_2} \sum_{s \in S} \theta_1^{(s)} \cdot \theta_2^{(s)} \cdot \left(\sigma^{(s)}\right)^2.$$

Proof. The correlation of the two random variables is defined as:

$$Cor(\tilde{I}_1, \tilde{I}_2) = \frac{Cov(\tilde{I}_1, \tilde{I}_2)}{\sqrt{V(\tilde{I}_1) \cdot V(\tilde{I}_2)}}.$$

For a small value of PD_i, the variance of $\tilde{I}_i$ can be approximated by:

$$V(\tilde{I}_i) = E(\tilde{I}_i^2) - E^2(\tilde{I}_i) = PD_i - PD_i^2 \approx PD_i$$

To obtain the covariance, define for convenience the random vector $\Psi = \left(\tilde{X}^{(1)}, \tilde{X}^{(2)}, \ldots\right)$. Then using the law of iterated expectations, the covariance can be computed as:[17]

$$\begin{aligned} Cov(\tilde{I}_1, \tilde{I}_2) &= E(\tilde{I}_1 \cdot \tilde{I}_2) - E(\tilde{I}_1) \cdot E(\tilde{I}_2) \\ &= E\left(E\left[\tilde{I}_1 \cdot \tilde{I}_2 | \Psi\right]\right) - E\left(E\left[\tilde{I}_1 | \Psi\right]\right) \cdot E\left(E\left[\tilde{I}_2 | \Psi\right]\right) \\ &= E\left(E\left[\tilde{I}_1 \cdot \tilde{I}_2 | \Psi\right]\right) - E\left\{\left(E\left[\tilde{I}_1 | \Psi\right]\right) \cdot E\left(E\left[\tilde{I}_2 | \Psi\right]\right)\right\} \\ &\quad + E\left\{\left(E\left[\tilde{I}_1 | \Psi\right]\right) \cdot E\left(E\left[\tilde{I}_2 | \Psi\right]\right)\right\} - E\left(E\left[\tilde{I}_1 | \Psi\right]\right) \cdot E\left(E\left[\tilde{I}_2 | \Psi\right]\right) \\ &= E\left(Cov\left[\tilde{I}_1, \tilde{I}_2 | \Psi\right]\right) + Cov\left(E\left[\tilde{I}_1 | \Psi\right], E\left[\tilde{I}_2 | \Psi\right]\right). \end{aligned}$$

Since $\tilde{I}_1$ and $\tilde{I}_2$ are conditionally independent, the first term can be set to zero. Due to the independence between the sectors, the second term can calculated as:

$$\begin{aligned} Cov\left(E\left[\tilde{I}_1 | \Psi\right], E\left[\tilde{I}_2 | \Psi\right]\right) &= Cov\left(\tilde{X}_1, \tilde{X}_2\right) \\ &= PD_1 \cdot PD_2 \cdot Cov\left(\sum_{s \in S} \theta_1^{(s)} \cdot \tilde{X}^{(s)}, \sum_{t \in S} \theta_2^{(t)} \cdot \tilde{X}^{(t)}\right) \\ &= PD_1 \cdot PD_2 \cdot \sum_{s \in S} \sum_{t \in S} \theta_1^{(s)} \cdot \theta_2^{(t)} \cdot Cov\left(\tilde{X}^{(s)}, \tilde{X}^{(t)}\right) \\ &= PD_1 \cdot PD_2 \cdot \sum_{s \in S} \theta_i^{(s)} \cdot \theta_j^{(s)} \cdot V\left(\tilde{X}^{(s)}\right). \end{aligned}$$

Plugging the variances and the covariances into the correlation formula completes the proof. ■

4.2.10 Discussion

Advantages and disadvantages of credit risk models in general have been discussed in the previous chapter within the context of requirements to be applied in the automotive industry.

[17] For the law of iterated expectations see, for example, Casella and Berger (2002), p. 164.

In this section, emphasis is placed on technical and empirical issues of CR+ in particular.[18]

Critical issues when employing CR+ can be separated according to their qualitative or quantitative characters. **Quantitative** issues are in particular the application of the Poisson approximation, and the transformation by infinite, gamma distributed random variables. These effects on the individual default probability $\tilde{X}_i$, however, can be neglected for sufficiently small average default probabilities PD_i.

Qualitative issues relate to assumptions which influence model forecast but cannot be empirically verified. Instead, only sensitivity analysis or stress testing may be possible. In CR+, such stress tests are possible for example by variation of the distribution of sector default rates. Gordy (2000) shows by simulation the impact of distribution assumptions in particular on the tail behavior of the loss distribution. However, only the choice of the gamma distribution ensures that the model can be analytically solved.

Some qualitative issues cannot be evaluated by stress tests, for example because underlying factors are unobservable. Such issues include the assumption of conditionally independent individual default rates and their functional form as well as the assumption of independent sectors. Furthermore, it has been criticized that there is no explicit dependency modeling. This argument can be countered by the observation that empirical results do not vary between models. In addition, dependencies in retail portfolios are generally difficult to quantify without means of expert knowledge.[19]

Although a simple at first glance, CR+ holds some distinct advantages in comparison to other credit risk models. First, the simplicity is in itself a strength, since it allows for easy implementation. The intuition behind the sector default rates also facilitates communication to senior management.[20] Additionally, the model offers fast calculation of the loss distribution and risk measures. This is also the case for large portfolios, scaling effects thus have much less influence in comparison to simulation models. Third, CR+ is parsimonious, i.e. it requires rel-

[18]For further discussions of CR+, see for example Crouhy et al. (2000), p. 113, Bürgisser et al. (1999), p. 1, or Bröker and Lehrbass (2001), p. 779. For critique see in particular Cossin and Pirotte (2004), p. 293, and Gordy (2000), p. 129.

[19]See section 4.2.9 for the correlations implied in CR+.

[20]A free Excel version is also available at http://www.csfb.com.

atively few inputs. This is an advantage for retail portfolios. For such borrowers, stock prices are not available to estimate PDs or correlations. Also, approaches toward calculating risk contributions are available. These are necessary in the suggested framework for credit securitization. Also, CR+ can be mapped to other models such as the well-known CreditMetrics™ or the model deployed by the Basle Committee for regulatory capital. Finally, the concepts behind CR+ are already well established in insurance.

To summarize, CR+ is a default mode model that makes few assumptions. Of these, the gamma distribution of the independent scaling factors is not replicable without loss of the analytical solvability. CR+ is a parsimonious model that can be implemented quickly. It allows for intuitive interpretation and is based on well-known concepts from the insurance industry. To conclude, CR+ poses a practical alternative for portfolios where rating changes need not be modeled.

4.3 Extensions of CreditRisk+

The basic CR+ model is still the object of intensive research, and many extensions of the original model have been developed. The different approaches are discussed in the following subsections.

4.3.1 Incorporation of Rating Migrations

The restriction of CR+ to the default as sole credit event can be a serious drawback for certain portfolios. Although it allows for a parsimonious model on the one hand, on the other hand it proscribes the application to portfolios of liquid instruments such as bonds: in that case the rating is crucial for the valuation. Rolfes and Broeker (1998) employ concepts from CreditMetrics™, and historical rating matrices in particular, to apply CR+ to bond portfolios without the need for Monte Carlo simulations.

First, as in CreditMetrics™, for each potential future rating class, appropriately discounted future values ("FV") are calculated for each bond. In the next step, by subtracting the FV of the bond for the current rating class, each rating class is assigned either a loss for a negative difference, or a gain for a positive difference. The main idea is then to view each of these differences as a distinct contract. Such a contract is assumed to have a PD equal to the transition probability from the current rating class, and an exposure equal to the difference. Since the current rating class has a difference of zero, it can be neglected. The remaining differences are then assigned to two sub-portfolios, one for the rating classes which imply a gain and the other for the rating classes which imply a loss. For these two sub-portfolios and the absolute values of both the gains and losses, the CR+ methodology is used to derive a gain and a loss distribution. These distributions are then convoluted to obtain the overall loss distribution.

The approach tackles a relevant problem which restricts the application of the analytical solution of CR+ to more liquid portfolios. The employment of transition matrices is well-known, for example from the CreditMetrics™ model. There are, however, two problems involved. First, by splitting a single instrument into a multitude of contracts corresponding to the different rating grades, the required computational time increases vastly. Whether this is pivotal depends on the size of the underlying portfolio. The second point relates to a formal inconsistency when modeling the conditionality of the defaults. Since rating grades are unique, the realization of a certain grade for a bond would imply that all other exposures relating to that bond, across the sub-portfolios, must "default". This is equivalent to setting the default rate of those exposures uniformly to one, which is not modeled. From this follows that more than one rating can be realized; the suggested approach is thus not valid. This problem is attenuated when the off-diagonal elements of the transition matrix are small.

4.3.2 Default and Loss Correlations

The assumption of independent sector scaling factors does not lend itself to intuition. This makes the distribution of exposures over the different sectors by the weights $\theta_i^{(s)}$, and thus the implementation of CR+, difficult: setting factor loadings is arbitrary and potentially time-consuming, and induces significant amounts of model risk. As an alternative, Bürgisser et al. (2001) suggest an extension of the basic model which allows for correlated sectors. Exposures are then uniquely assigned to sectors, and the dependence of default rates and of the defaults is the result of the dependencies between the sectors.

In addition to correlated default rate sectors, the article suggests an approach toward modeling stochastic and correlated loss rates. Both extensions are based on the observation that the variance of portfolio loss cannot be uniquely assigned to a specific form of the loss distribution. In this section, the model is first introduced, followed by the variance formulae. Based on these, finally the construction of the loss distribution is outlined. The model is simple and fast, and allows the issue of volatile and correlated loss rates to be tackled. The latter is of crucial importance in the automotive industry.

Setting

In addition to the s default rate sectors S^s with sector default rate $\widetilde{X}^{(s)}$, the model contains r loss rate segments L^r with segment loss rate $\widetilde{Y}^{(r)}$. Both default and loss rates are of mean one and utilize the same mechanism to scale the individual rates. They are pairwise independent, but can be separately dependent among the loss and default rates with correlation $Cor\left(\widetilde{X}^{(s)}, \widetilde{X}^{(t)}\right)$ and $Cor\left(\widetilde{Y}^{(r)}, \widetilde{Y}^{(u)}\right)$, respectively. Instead by means of sector weights, dependencies are directly modeled. Thus, borrowers can be uniquely assigned to an intersection of default rate sector and loss rate segment.

To calculate the individual loss of borrower i, the original model's standardized exposure ν_i net of recovery must be split into outstanding ϵ_i and realized individual recovery $\widetilde{LGD}_i$: $\nu_i = \epsilon_i \cdot \widetilde{LGD}_i$. $\widetilde{LGD}_i$ is modeled as the product of two random variables, the segment factor $\widetilde{Y}^{(r)}$ and a borrower-specific severity $\widetilde{l}_i$: $\widetilde{LGD}_i = \widetilde{l}_i \cdot \widetilde{Y}^{(r)}$. Thus, portfolio loss is given by:

$$\widetilde{L} = \sum_s \sum_r \sum_{i \in I} I_{\{i \in S^{(s)} \cap L^{(r)}\}} \cdot \widetilde{I}_i \cdot \epsilon_i \cdot \widetilde{l}_i \cdot \widetilde{Y}^{(r)}$$

where $\widetilde{I}_i$ is a Bernoulli variable with parameter $\widetilde{X}_i = PD_i \cdot \widetilde{X}^{(s)}$ for each borrower belonging to default rate sector s.

Calculation of the Second Central Moment

To calculate the moments of the loss distribution, let $\sigma^{(s)}$ and $\delta^{(r)}$ denote the standard deviations of default rate sector s and loss rate segment r, respectively. δ_i is the standard deviation of the individual loss rate of borrower i. Further, use the following definitions for partial unconditional expected losses:

$$\begin{aligned} EL^{(s,r)} &= \sum_{i \in I} I_{\{i \in S^{(s)} \cap L^{(r)}\}} PD_i \cdot \nu_i \\ EL^{(s)} &= \sum_r EL^{(s,r)} \\ EL^{(r)} &= \sum_s EL^{(s,r)} \end{aligned}$$

Then Bürgisser et al. (2001) prove the following formula for the variance of total losses, regardless of the underlying distribution of the risk drivers.

Theorem 3 (Bürgisser et al. (2001),p. 10) *The variance of the unconditional loss distribution can be split into two factors:*

$$V\left(\widetilde{L}\right) = \sigma_{syst}^2 + \sigma_{div}^2 \tag{4.3}$$

The variance due to systematic risk σ_{syst}^2 is given by:

$$\begin{aligned} \sigma_{syst}^2 &= \sum_{s,t} Cor\left(\widetilde{X}^{(s)}, \widetilde{X}^{(t)}\right) \sigma^{(s)} \sigma^{(t)} EL^{(s)} EL^{(t)} \\ &+ \sum_{r,u} Cor\left(\widetilde{Y}^{(r)}, \widetilde{Y}^{(u)}\right) \delta^{(r)} \delta^{(u)} EL^{(s)} EL^{(t)} \\ &+ \sum_{s,t} \sum_{r,u} Cor\left(\widetilde{X}^{(s)}, \widetilde{X}^{(t)}\right) \sigma^{(s)} \sigma^{(t)} Cor\left(\widetilde{Y}^{(r)}, \widetilde{Y}^{(u)}\right) \delta^{(r)} \delta^{(u)} EL^{(s)} EL^{(t)} \end{aligned}$$

The variance amount which can be diversified σ_{div}^2 is given by:

$$\sigma_{div}^2 = \sum_r \left(1 + \delta^{(r)^2}\right) \sum_s \sum_{i \in S^{(s)} \cap L^{(r)}} \left[\left(1 + \delta_i^2\right) PD_i - \left(1 + \left(\sigma^{(s)}\right)^2\right) PD_i^2\right] \epsilon_i^2$$

The first two terms of σ_{syst}^2 can be interpreted as systematic risk due to default and loss rate volatility, respectively. The third term represents the joint influence of the two risk drivers. Regarding σ_{div}^2, Bürgisser et al. (2001) show in a second theorem the declining influence of the diversifiable variance portion.

Calculation of Loss Distribution

Bürgisser et al. (2001) observe that, due to the functional form of equation 4.3, p. 56, the variance of total portfolio loss does not depend on the functional form of the loss distribution, but exclusively on borrower, sector, and segment parameters. To derive the loss distribution for a given combination of sectors and segments, they suggest calculating in a first step the expected loss and variance for that setting. In the second step, these two parameters are employed to construct the loss distribution in a more basic setting. For simplicity, this may involve either only one default rate sector or only one loss rate segment.[21]

4.4 Implementation of CreditRisk+

4.4.1 Determination of Loss Distribution

Derivation of Loss Distribution- The Original Approach

The standard way to derive the mass function from a PGF $G(z)$ is to compute appropriate derivatives, which follows from the definition of the PGF.[22] Although trivial from a theoretical point of view, there is no closed solution for the derivatives which can be used for automatic calculation. A manual calculation is for realistic portfolios not tractable due to the high derivatives and large ν_i involved.

As an alternative, the recursion relation developed in Panjer (1981) can be employed. Let $G(z)$ denote the total loss PGF, and assume that the following derivative exists:

$$\frac{d}{dz}\left[\ln G(z)\right] = \frac{1}{G(z)} \cdot \frac{dG(z)}{dz} = \frac{a_0 + a_1 z^1 + ... + a_r z^r}{b_0 + b_1 z^1 + ... + b_s z^s} = \frac{A(z)}{B(z)}.$$

Then the probabilities of the random variable $\tilde{L}$ which describes total portfolio loss can be

[21] (See Bürgisser et al., 2001, p. 17).

[22] See section 4.2.1.

calculated as follows:[23]

$$P\left(\tilde{L}=0\right) = F(0)$$

$$P\left(\tilde{L}=n+1\right) = \frac{1}{b_0 \cdot (n+1)} \left[\sum_{i=0}^{\min(r,n)} a_i \cdot A_{n-i} - \sum_{j=0}^{\min(s-1,n-1)} b_{j+1} \cdot (n-j) \cdot A_{n-j} \right]$$

The derivative of the log of the total loss PGF in CR+ can be computed as follows: [24]

$$\frac{\partial}{\partial z}\left[\ln G(z)\right] = \sum_{s \in S} \left[\frac{\frac{\alpha^{(s)} \cdot \delta^{(s)}}{\mu^{(s)}} \cdot \sum_{i \in I} \theta_i^{(s)} \cdot PD_i \cdot \nu_i \cdot z^{\nu_i - 1}}{1 - \frac{\delta^{(s)}}{\mu^{(s)}} \cdot \sum_{i \in I} \theta_i^{(s)} \cdot PD_i \cdot z^{\nu_i}} \right] = \frac{A(z)}{B(z)} \tag{4.4}$$

If idiosyncratic sectors are used, the following form is obtained:

$$\sum_{i \in I} \nu_i \cdot PD_i \cdot \theta_i^{(0)} \cdot z^{\nu_i - 1} + \sum_{s \in S} \left[\frac{\frac{\alpha^{(s)} \cdot \delta^{(s)}}{\mu^{(s)}} \sum_{i \in I} \theta_i^{(s)} \cdot PD_i \cdot \nu_i \cdot z^{\nu_i - 1}}{1 - \frac{\delta^{(s)}}{\mu^{(s)}} \cdot \sum_{i \in I} \theta_i^{(s)} \cdot PD_i \cdot z^{\nu_i}} \right] = \frac{A(z)}{B(z)}$$

Thus, to compute the loss distribution from the PGF, the coefficients of the two polynomials $A(z)$ and $B(z)$ have to be computed. For the implementation of the model, Wilde (1997b) suggests the following recurrence summation procedure: Let T_i and $Q_i, i = 1, ..., m$ denote the nominator and the denominator of the ith factor of the sum in 4.4, and T and Q help polynomials for the moving factor sums. Then the following pseudo-code describes how the polynomials $A(z)$ and $B(z)$ can be derived from the PGF.

1. Set $T = T_1, Q = Q_1$.

2. For $i = 2, ..., m$ set:

$$T = T \cdot Q_i + Q \cdot Ti$$
$$Q = Q \cdot Q_i$$

   Next i.

3. Set $A(z) = T$ and $B(z) = Q$.

In step 2, it is important to do the calculations of T and Q in exactly the sequence given above. If an idiosyncratic factor is used, the algorithm is initiated with $T = \sum_{i \in I} \nu_i \cdot PD_i \cdot \theta_i^{(0)} \cdot z^{\nu_i - 1}$ and $Q = 1$.

[23] Exact calculations are given in the appendix. Note that for $P(L=1)$ the second sum is zero.

[24] Exact calculations are given in the appendix.

Problem Checks for the Original Approach

Different determinants rule the applicability of the Panjer relation to calculate the mass distribution from the PGF. Whereas the calculation speed depends on the effective implementation of the recursive summation algorithm and the choice of the standardization unit, the algorithm itself might not be computationally stable due to subtractive cancellation.[25] Subtractive cancellation in addition operations occurs due to rounding errors induced by computer arithmetics. The effects can be formalized by introducing the relative error ϵ_x of a numerical value x, which is defined as the percentage of the correct value x on the value x_c used by the computer: $\epsilon_x = \frac{x_c}{x}$. For two numerical values x and y the relative error of $z = x + y \neq 0$ is given by:

$$\epsilon_z = \frac{x\epsilon_x + y\epsilon_y}{x+y} = \frac{x}{x+y}\epsilon_x + \frac{y}{x+y}\epsilon_y$$

If both x and y are of positive sign, the relative error of ϵ_z cannot be larger than $max\,(\epsilon_x, \epsilon_y)$. If both deviate in sign, the relative error can in contrast increase.

Given that the factors in the polynomials T and Q can vary in sign, the repeated summing can lead to massive rounding errors induced by subtractive cancellation of terms with similar magnitude but opposite signs. This effect can be critical especially in the tails of the distribution, and may even result in negative probabilities for high quantiles. Since the number of addition operations is contingent on the magnitude of the standardized exposures, the enhanced precision induced by a smaller standardization unit L might thus be counteracted by an increase in rounding error. Effects can be worsened by a higher number of sectors, which boosts the number of summations. Gordy (2001a), p. 7, finds that the Panjer algorithm can break down for as few as seven risk factors and 5000 obligors.

As a general check for both implementation and calculation problems, Gordy (2001a) suggests comparing mean, variance, skewness, and kurtosis of the loss distributions as implied by the Panjer recursion, on the one hand, and by the corresponding cumulant generating function ("CGF") on the other.[26] CGFs possess two distinct advantages in comparison to PGFs. First,

[25] See for example Gordy (2001a) or Haaf et al. (2002).

[26] For an initial introduction to CGFs, see Casella and Berger (2002) , p. 83. An extensive discussion is as always in Stuart and Ord (1994). CGFs are also discussed in the next section.

they allow for a faster calculation of the moments with regard to both the number of sectors and the size of the standardization unit.[27] Second, the approach is robust with regard to the standardization unit L. Hence, significant differences between the two approaches can indicate that, for example, the recurrence algorithm or the standardization unit is flawed. Rules of thumb on when to regard the algorithm as flawed are given in the article.

Saddlepoint Approximation of Quantiles

Gordy (2001a) suggests an alternative approach to deriving the loss distribution. The saddlepoint approach allows quantiles of the loss distribution to be approximated without explicitly calculating the overall distribution. Saddlepoint approximations are based on the CGF. As the PGF, the CGF is an alternative representation of the density respective mass function, which are convenient especially for the computation of moments. Different formulae can be applied for saddlepoint approximations, a popular example being the Lugannani-Rice formula introduced in this section.[28] Other well-known approximations seem to be less robust, or do not improve the performance in the context of CR+.[29]

The CGF $C(z)$ of a random variable X with PGF $F(z)$ is defined as:

$$C(z) = \ln E\left([exp(z)]^X\right) = \ln F\left(exp(z)\right)$$

The derivatives of a CGF evaluated at $z = 0$ are the cumulants from which moments of the distribution can be computed. For example, if κ_n denotes the nth cumulant, then $E(X) = \kappa_1$ and $V(X) = \kappa_2$. The skewness and the kurtosis of a random variable can be related similarly to the cumulants, if more involved. In CR+, from the PGF of total loss $F(z)$ the CGF of total

[27](See Gordy, 2001a, p. 37).

[28]For more information on saddlepoint approximations and alternative formulae see for example Feuerverger and Wong (2000) or Studer (2001).

[29](See Gordy, 2001a, pp. 1348–1349).

loss $C(z)$ can be derived:

$$\begin{aligned} C(z) &= \ln F(\exp(z)) \\ &= \sum_{i\in I} PD_i \cdot \theta_i^{(0)} \cdot \exp(z)^{\nu_i} - \sum_{i\in I} PD_i \cdot \theta_i^{(0)} \\ &\quad + \sum_{s\in S} \alpha^{(s)} \cdot \ln\left(\frac{1-\delta^{(s)}}{1-\frac{\delta^{(s)}}{\mu^{(s)}} \cdot \sum_{i\in I} \theta_i^{(s)} \cdot PD_i \cdot \exp(z\nu_i)}\right) \end{aligned}$$

The Lugannani-Rice formula to approximate quantiles of a probability distribution with CGF $C(z)$ and cumulative distribution function $G(x)$ is then given by:

$$1 - G(y) = q \approx 1 - \Phi(w) + \phi(w)\left(\frac{1}{u} - \frac{1}{w}\right),$$

where

$$\begin{aligned} w &= \sqrt{2\left(\widehat{z} \cdot y - C(\widehat{z})\right)} \\ u &= \widehat{z} \cdot \sqrt{C''(\widehat{z})} \end{aligned}$$

and the saddlepoint $\widehat{z}$ solves $C'(z) = y$. $\Phi()$ and $\phi()$ are the standard normal cumulative distribution and density function, respectively. This approximation is discussed in detail in Lugannani and Rice (1980), and is, for example, used in Feuerverger and Wong (2000) to compute the market value at risk of a large portfolio.

To approximate the quantile y for a given $q \in [0,1]$, it is suggested to compute a sufficiently fine grid of pairs $(1 - G(y), z)$ using the above approximation. This results in a matrix such as depicted in table 4.1, where interpolations can be employed to approximate y. As Gordy (2001a) points out, the saddlepoint $\widehat{z}$ must exist. To further facilitate calculations, the range of z can be restricted if for the chosen quantile $q \geq C(E[L])$. As the article shows, $z \in \left(0, \min_s \left(l^{(s)}\right)\right]$, where:

$$l^{(s)} = \frac{-\ln \delta_{(s)}}{\sum_{i\in I} \nu_i \cdot \frac{\theta_i^{(s)} \cdot PD_i}{\mu^{(s)}}}$$

The saddlepoint approximation allows a fast and relatively robust approximation of the quantiles of the loss distribution. Additionally, it is insensitive to the choice of the standardization unit and the trade-off regarding computational time. Nor do problems regarding subtrac-

z	$y =$	$w =$	$u =$	$q \approx$
0	$C'(0)$	$\sqrt{2\left(\widehat{z} \cdot y - C\left(\widehat{z}\right)\right)}$	$u = \widehat{z} \cdot \sqrt{C''\left(\widehat{z}\right)}$	$\Phi(w) + \phi(w)\left(\frac{1}{u} - \frac{1}{w}\right)$
...	...	...	...	...
$\min_s\left(l^{(s)}\right)$	$C'\left(min_s l^{(s)}\right)$	$\sqrt{2\left(\widehat{z} \cdot y - C\left(\widehat{z}\right)\right)}$	$u = \widehat{z} \cdot \sqrt{C''\left(\widehat{z}\right)}$	$\Phi(w) + \phi(w)\left(\frac{1}{u} - \frac{1}{w}\right)$

Table 4.1: Calculation Scheme

tive cancellation arise. The popularity of this approach is also reflected by the introduction of a second model, "PortfolioRisk+", by CreditSuisse: this model is fully based on the concept.

Regarding the disadvantages, it is difficult to evaluate the quality of the approximation. As Feuerverger and Wong (2000), p. 43, point out, "it is difficult to provide a simple intuitive explanation ... for the exceptional effectiveness of the saddlepoint approximation". Martin et al. (2001a) find, in a study, that the approach performs badly for undiversified portfolios. Gordy (2001a) concludes that the Panjer algorithm and the saddlepoint approximation support each other, i.e. the former should be used for smaller, undiversified portfolios, and the latter for larger, diversified ones. Generally, support for the quality of the approach is anecdotal, which is also the case for the choice of the different formulae. Finally, saddlepoint approximations focus on the estimation of quantiles, and the construction of the complete distribution of these is not feasible. Thus, advanced and in particular coherent risk measures as opposed to the value at risk cannot be calculated.

Nested Calculation

The nested calculation is an alternative scheme to obtain the discrete loss probabilities. It is based on a reformulation of the total loss PGF which avoids the problem of subtractive cancellation. By using power series approximations it is exact up to a to-be-defined factor.[30]

Starting point for the nested calculation is an alternative formulation of the loss distribution which can be derived from 1 on page 150 in the Appendix. The total loss PGF for the model

[30] See Giese (2003) and Haaf et al. (2002).

including idiosyncratic sectors can be reformulated as:

$$\begin{aligned} G(z) &= \exp\left(\left[\sum_{i\in I} PD_i \cdot \theta_i^{(0)}\right] \cdot (z^{\nu_i} - 1)\right) \\ &\quad \prod_s \left(1 - \beta^{(s)} \cdot \sum_{i\in I} \theta_i^{(s)} \cdot PD_i \cdot z^{\nu_i} + \beta^{(s)} \cdot \mu^{(s)}\right)^{-\alpha^{(s)}} \\ &= \exp\left(P^{(0)}(z) - P^{(0)}(1) - \sum_s \alpha^{(s)} \ln\left[1 - \beta^{(s)} \cdot P^{(s)}(z) + \beta^{(s)} \cdot P^{(s)}(1)\right]\right) \qquad (4.5) \\ &= \sum_{k=0}^{\infty} P(L = k)\, z^k \end{aligned}$$

where

$$P^{(s)}(z) = \sum_{i\in I} PD_i \cdot \theta_i^{(s)} z^{\nu_i}$$

Haaf et al. (2002) suggest a two-step procedure in which the logarithm is first expanded using its power series representation. For the expansion, the authors employ the following lemma which holds under very general assumptions regarding the function $f()$.

Lemma 4 (Haaf et al. (2002), pg. 4) *Let (a_k) be a sequence with $a > 0$ and $a_k \geq 0$ $(k \geq 1)$, and define:*

$$\begin{aligned} f(z) &:= \sum_{k=1}^{\infty} a_k z^k \\ g(z) &:= -\ln(a_0 - f(z)) \end{aligned}$$

Then $g(z)$ has a power series representation $g(z) = \sum_{k=1}^{\infty} b_k z^k$ with $b_k \geq 0\,(k \geq 1)$. The coefficients can be computed recursively and numerically stable by:

$$\begin{aligned} b_0 &= -\ln(a_0) \\ b_k &= \frac{1}{a_0}\left[a_k + \frac{1}{k}\sum_{q=1}^{k-1} q b_q a_{k-q}\right] \end{aligned}$$

The proof is straightforward, the stability follows from the positivity of (a_k).

By constructing the sequence $\left(a_k^{(s)}\right)$ as follows, the logarithms corresponding to the sectors $s \in S$ in 4.5 can be calculated. This construction also ensures that all a_k are non-negative.[31]

$$\begin{aligned} a_0^{(s)} &= 1 + \beta^{(s)} \cdot P^{(s)}(1) \\ a_k^{(s)} &= \beta^{(s)} \sum_{i \in I} PD_i \cdot \theta_i^{(s)} I_{\nu_i = k} \end{aligned}$$

From these, using the lemma above, the coefficients $b_k^{(s)}$ from the corresponding power series can be calculated:

$$\ln\left[1 - \beta^{(s)} \cdot P^{(s)}(z) + \beta^{(s)} \cdot P^{(s)}(1)\right] = \sum_{k=1}^{\infty} b_k^{(s)} z^k = \sum_{k=1}^{M} b_k^{(s)} z^k + O\left(z^{M+1}\right)$$

Here $O()$ denotes the remaining polynomial factors not included in the sum. M is the maximal exponent of the power series, which determines the degree up to which the probabilities are exact. With regard to its size, it is suggested to set $M = \sum_i \nu_i$.

Summing up the coefficients of the power series across all sectors after multiplying with $\alpha^{(s)}$ and adding $P^{(0)}(z) - P^{(0)}(1)$, the PGF can be expressed as:[32]

$$G(z) = \exp\left(\sum_{k=0}^{\infty} c_k z^k\right)$$

To solve the exponential function for the final polynomial presentation, the following lemma can be used.

Lemma 5 (Haaf et al. (2002), pg. 5) *Let a sequence* (a_k) *be defined as in the previous lemma. Define:*

$$\begin{aligned} f(z) &:= \sum_{k=0}^{\infty} a_k z^k \\ g(z) &:= exp(f(z)) \end{aligned}$$

[31] Note that the result of this computation is a single power series for each sector.

[32] If idiosyncratic sectors are used, negative cancellation might occur when the coefficients of $P^{(0)}(z)$ are subtracted.

Then $g(z)$ can be expressed as power series $g(z) = \sum_{k=0}^{\infty} b_k z^k$ and the coefficients can be computed numerically stable as:

$$\begin{aligned} b_0 &= exp(a_0) \\ b_n &= \sum_{k=1}^{\infty} \frac{k}{n} b_{n-k} a_k \end{aligned}$$

The lemma can be applied by setting $a_k = c_k$ to obtain

$$G(z) = \sum_{k=1}^{M} P(L = k) z^k + O\left(z^{M+1}\right)$$

Haaf et al. (2002), p. 6, also give a formula for the number of calculation operations which can be used to evaluate processing time.

Application of Characteristic Function

Reiß (2003) suggests an alternative derivation of the total loss distribution based on the inversion of the characteristic function. This approach also avoids subtractive cancellation and the problems involved in choosing the standardized loss unit L. Since the classical approach using the Fourier inversion is not applicable due to the discrete distribution of losses, he suggests two approximation procedures: the fast Fourier transformation and a density approximation based on the matching of moments.[33]

4.4.2 Further Issues

Value of Standardization Unit

In the original derivation of CR+ rounding exposures to the nearest integer is suggested.[34] Two reasons are put forward for a restriction to rounding up. First, rounding in both directions might, for sufficiently small exposures, result in a standardized exposure of zero. Second, from a risk management point of view it is usually preferable to obtain more conservative estimates, which imply an increase, rather than a decrease of the exposures.

[33](See Reiß, 2003, p. 9).

[34](See Wilde, 1997b, p. 36).

When either rounding or standardizing the exposures, the expected loss based on the original parameters becomes difficult to align with the risk measures based on the standardized parameters. Wilde (1997b), p. 36, suggests that "an adjustment to the default probabilities to preserve the expected losses is made" without further specification. In the empirical part of this thesis in chapter 7, all risk measures including the expected loss are computed on the basis of the standardized risk parameters.

Interpretation and Choice of Sectors

The interpretation of sector parameters in CR+ can be best understood by analyzing the basic implementation, where all contracts are assigned to a single sector. The risk driver of this sector $\widetilde{X}^{(s)}$ can then be interpreted as the influence of the whole economy on default probabilities. In this case, if, for example, the risk driver is relatively high, the same holds for the individual default. [35]

The interpretation of a single sector as global influence translates to the case of multiple sectors, which may represent different industries, for example. It is, however, difficult from a practical point of view to assume such background factors as independent. This problem can be mitigated in three ways. First, it is possible to assign exposures simultaneously to different sectors; this equivalent to assuming a factor model for the individual default rates. The second mitigation is a modified version of the basic CR+ model which allows correlated sectors and has been described in the previous section. Finally, Boegelein et al. (2002) have suggested an approach to determine independent sectors by conditioning on macro-economic factors and employing seemingly unrelated regression.

With regard to loss rate segments in Bürgisser et al. (2001), these can be interpreted as representing, for example, different vehicle classes in automobile portfolios. Classes such as luxury and heavy utility vehicles can be expected to have different used car price volatilities. Yet, there should also exist correlations between prices across used car markets. The empirical analysis in chapter 7 targets this interpretation by applying a vehicle classification. Additional

[35](See Lehrbass et al., 2001, p. 14).

loss rate drivers such as recollection and remarketing costs are neglected due to insufficient data.

Concerning the parametrization of the sector and segment random variables of the underlying gamma distributions, the initial approach in Wilde (1997a) was to estimate the sector mean and variance from the borrowers' PDs and variances as weighted sum.[36] As an alternative, Boegelein et al. (2002) suggest an approach for parameter estimation based on a macroeconomic regression-type model.

4.5 The Regulatory Model

Basle II offers three different approaches in all for the calculation of regulatory capital. These can be separated into the standardized approach and a foundation and an advanced internal ratings-based approach ("IRB"). All three approaches have the same simple underlying model. The approaches differ, however, with regard to the inputs estimated by the bank. No internal estimates can be employed in the standardized approach. In the foundation IRB approach banks can estimate probabilities of default and, in the advanced IRB approach, the risk parameters PD, LGD, and EAD. A general differentiation is required between corporate and retail exposures, regarding in particular the inclusion of the expected loss in the capital requirements or maturity adjustments. As far as these are concerned, retail portfolios are considered to be of higher granularity and shorter maturity.

The model underlying the Basle II capital requirements is presented, for example, in Gordy (2001b). The theoretical underpinning has not been modified over the different Basle II consultation papers. Instead, the focus in the different versions has been on recalibrating input factors. This is possible because calibration formulae are not model-based. As an example, correlations are functions of the respective probabilities of default. It further indicates that emphasis lies less on modeling and more on parameter specification.

The motivations behind the changing of the consultative papers were two-fold. First, it is a declared goal of the Basle Committee to keep total capital requirements at 8% of the portfolio

[36](See also Wilde, 1997b, p. 43).

volume, as has been the requirement under Basle I. This is to be achieved by a trial-and-error process- based on experience collected, for example, in the course of the quantitative impact studies. Second, the awareness of the insufficiencies of the underlying model have originally motivated additional factors accounting for maturities, concentration risks or small portfolio sizes. These have been partly removed with the intention to avoid unnecessary complications.

The underlying credit risk model estimates the loss distribution of the portfolio in one year; regulatory capital requirements are set at the 99.9% quantile. The model is based on the stochastic of the asset value. Default occurs when this variable passes a certain lower treshold. It is assumed that the default events are mutually dependent based on a single latent factor, and independent conditional on it. Regarding the portfolio as a whole, it is assumed to be of infinite granularity. The model for standardized asset value changes Y_i of exposure i, based on the common factor Z, is then given by:

$$Y_i = \omega_i Z + \sqrt{1 - \omega_i^2} U_i \quad (\omega_i \in [-1, 1])$$

Dependencies between defaults are modeled by ω_i, which are weights of the common factor Z. U_i is an individual factor, accounting for borrower-specific asset value changes.

Two assumptions are necessary regarding the stochastic of the random variables. First, all random variables Z and U_i $(i = 1, \ldots, K)$ follow a standard normal distribution. Second, they are all pairwise independent. In this case, the Y_i follow a standard normal distribution as well, and correlations between Y_i and $Y_k (k \neq i)$ are given by:

$$\rho_{Y_i, Y_k} = \omega_i \omega_k \quad (i \neq k)$$

Next, a default indicator variable A_i is defined. It is assumed to have a Bernoulli distribution with parameter PD_i, equal to the probability of default estimated by the bank. Default occurs when the asset value differences goes below a certain minimum d_i. Thus, for PD_i the following relation must hold:

$$PD_i = P(A_i = 1) = P(Y_i \leq d_i) \Leftrightarrow d_i = \Phi^{-1}(PD_i)$$

The last equation follows due to the distributional assumptions, where $\Phi(x)$ denotes a standard normal cumulative distribution function. If z is a specific realization of the common factor Z, the conditional default probability $p_i(z)$ of customer i is deterministic and can be derived as:

$$\begin{aligned} p_i(z) := P\left(A_i = 1|Z = z\right) &= P\left[\omega_i z + \sqrt{1-\omega_i^2}U_i \leq \Phi^{-1}\left(PD_i\right)|Z = z\right] \quad (4.6) \\ &= P\left[U_i \leq \frac{\Phi^{-1}(PD_i) - \omega_i z}{\sqrt{1-\omega_i^2}}|Z = z\right] \\ &= \Phi\left(\frac{\Phi^{-1}(PD_i) - \omega_i z}{\sqrt{1-\omega_i^2}}|Z = z\right) \end{aligned}$$

To compute aggregate portfolio losses, let $b_i \in [0,1]$ with $\sum_{i=1}^K b_i = 1$ define the percentage exposure of customer i on the whole portfolio. Further, let LGD_i denote the related loss rate. Then given that the random variables A_i are conditionally independent, the conditional portfolio loss L, its mean and variance are given by:

$$\begin{aligned} L &= \sum_{i=1}^{K} b_i A_i LGD_i \\ E\left(L|Z\right) &= \sum_{i=1}^{K} p_i(z) b_i LGD_i \\ V\left(L|Z\right) &= \sum_{i=1}^{K} p_i(z)\left(1 - PD_i(z)\right) b_i^2 LGD_i^2 \\ &\leq \sum_{i=1}^{K} b_i^2 \end{aligned}$$

The variance becomes infinitely small and can be neglected under the assumption of an infinitely grained portfolio. In such a portfolio, no single dominating exposure exists, and $K \to \infty$. This is, for example, the case for large K and $b_i = 1/K$. Using this approximation, by prescribing a realization of Z equal to the desired quantile of 99.9%, regulatory capital requirements can be calculated. In this basic model, required inputs are the three risk parameters loss rate, exposure and default rate as well as the correlation factor ω_i for each contract.

A feature of crucial importance to the regulators in this model is the availability of "risk buckets".[37] That is, capital requirements for each contract can be calculated separately, independent of the portfolio context. Among others, this reason has made the Basle II model very

[37] See Finger (2001), p. 10, and Gordy (2001b).

popular among practitioners. Other reasons for its attractiveness are the compatibility with regulatory requirements and its easy implementation, avoiding the question of how to model and estimate default dependencies for example. A final observation in favor of the regulatory model is its relation to the two popular credit risk models CreditMetrics and CR+.[38]

On the other hand, the regulatory model and its application for the setting of capital requirements are also prone to criticism. Regarding the model itself, the negligence of concentration risks by assuming infinitely grained portfolios is not realistic. Additionally, the interpretation of the common factor Z is difficult. This includes the question of whether the implied uniform random walk is indeed representative for all periods of the credit cycle. Concerning its application to the setting of credit requirements, the question arises as to why internal models should not be utilized where available. These could be expected to be both advanced and adjusted to local requirements, in comparison to the simple regulatory model based on very strict assumptions. Moreover, further criticism can be raised as to the parametrization of the model, which is ad hoc and not based on theoretical considerations.

---

[38] See Finger (1998), Koyluoglu and Hickman (1998) or Gordy (2000).

Chapter 5

Credit Risk Management

The goal of credit risk management is to maximize a bank's risk-adjusted rate of return by maintaining credit risk exposure within acceptable parameters.

BIS (2000), p. 1

The above quotation well summarizes the basic concept of credit risk management. Based on this general objective, credit risk management relates to different fields such as credit decisions, risk-based pricing, risk controlling, and portfolio risk management.[1] The purpose of this thesis is the analysis of securitization as a means for portfolio risk management. This requires a thorough understanding of how risk can be measured, and how much each individual asset in a portfolio contributes. These two issues are analyzed in this chapter which focuses on credit risk. Risk measures and contributions are examined both in general and for the particular case where CreditRisk+ is the underlying credit risk model.

5.1 Risk Measures and Contributions

5.1.1 Portfolio Risk Measures

The risks of a portfolio are fully described by the loss distribution. Since the loss distribution as a whole is often difficult to interpret, risk management usually targets at a single one-

[1](See Wilde, 1997b, p. 28).

dimensional risk measure ρ. As an example, ρ can be constructed as a high quantile of the loss distribution representing economic capital ("EC").[2] The computation of a portfolio risk measure is also necessary to evaluate individual risk contributions.

Concerning the construction of a risk measure, theory and practice have diverged since the measures currently employed in practice are formally suboptimal. The academic requirements have been developed in the path-breaking article written by Artzner et al. (1999), who provides four attributes of an optimal risk measure. A risk measure ρ meeting all four attributes is then called a coherent measure. In the following, $\tilde{L}_i$ $(i \in \{1,2\})$ denotes the loss of portfolio i.[3]

Definition 3 (Coherent Risk Measures) *A risk measure $\rho()$ is called coherent if it possesses the following attributes:*

1. ***Translation Invariance***

$$\rho\left(\tilde{L}_1 + x\right) = \rho\left(\tilde{L}_1\right) - x \qquad (x \in \mathbb{R})$$

2. ***Subadditivity***

$$\rho\left(\tilde{L}_1 + \tilde{L}_2\right) \leq \rho\left(\tilde{L}_1\right) + \rho\left(\tilde{L}_2\right)$$

3. ***Positive Homogeneity***

$$\rho\left(x \cdot \tilde{L}_1\right) = x \cdot \rho\left(\tilde{L}_1\right) \qquad (x \geq 0)$$

4. ***Monotonicity***

$$\tilde{L}_1 \geq \tilde{L}_2 \; a.s. \Leftrightarrow \rho\left(\tilde{L}_1\right) \geq \rho\left(\tilde{L}_2\right)$$

These four attributes can be interpreted economically. First, translation invariance refers to the inclusion of risk-free assets, which should decrease risk. Second, subadditivity implies that the risk measure should allow for diversification. Third, positive homogeneity means that the

[2]See the next chapter for a discussion of economic and regulatory capital.

[3]The following definition is taken from Frey and McNeil (2002) and is adjusted for portfolios containing credit risk.

multiple of a certain risk implies the same multiple of the risk measure. Finally, monotonicity requires that higher risks be indicated by higher values of the risk measure.[4]

5.1.2 Examples for Portfolio Risk Measures

The expected loss, i.e. the expected value of the loss distribution, is the most popular traditional risk measure. To emphasize the importance of losses exceeding the mean the generic term unexpected losses has been introduced. Examples of such measures for the unexpected loss described in the literature are the variance, or derivations thereof, the Value at Risk ("VaR") and the expected shortfall.[5] Of these three, the traditional measure of individual and portfolio risk is the standard deviation $\rho^{SD}(\tilde{L})$. This risk measure is generally not coherent, since it is not monotonous. This is intuitive, as the scale parameter can overcompensate the location parameter. Moreover, the variance does not distinguish between loss risk and opportunity, i.e. between positive and negative deviations.

If the loss distribution is normal, a quantile risk measure can be constructed by adding multiples of the standard deviation to the mean. For general distributions, assuming that both mean and variance exist, the one-sided Chebycheff inequality can be used.[6] Let $\tilde{L}$ denote total portfolio loss with standard deviation $\rho^{SD}(\tilde{L})$ and mean μ_L, and let $x > 0$ and $\alpha \in (0, 1)$ be close to zero, then the following equation holds:

$$P\left(\tilde{L} \geq \mu_L + x \cdot \rho^{SD}(\tilde{L})\right) \leq \frac{1}{x^2+1} = \alpha$$

Setting $x_\alpha = \sqrt{(1-\alpha)/\alpha}$, the following risk measure $\rho^{Cheb}(L)$ approximates the α quantile of the underlying loss distribution:

$$\rho^{Cheb}(\tilde{L}) = \mu_L + x_\alpha \cdot \sigma_L$$

[4]Further criteria can also be thought of, e.g. distributional invariance. This describes the requirement that identical distributions for $\tilde{L}_1$ and $\tilde{L}_2$ should yield the same realization of the risk measure.

[5]In practice, regulatory capital is also used as risk measure. Currently, there are efforts to develop a more risk-sensitive framework Basle II. Under the old system, banks are required to hold approximately 8% of the exposure.

[6](See Casella and Berger, 2002, p. 122).

By providing the (physical) capital of $\rho^{Cheb}(\tilde{L})$, a financial institution is safe from illiquidity due to losses $(1-\alpha)\%$ of the time. This approximation, however, can be very crude, resulting in excessively large risk measures.

VaR is currently the market standard and has also been applied in the regulatory framework.[7] It is defined as an appropriate quantile of the loss distribution. Hence, the VaR is set equal to a loss that is not exceeded with a high probability. In the literature, the term is not employed consistently but often being used interchangeable with unexpected loss. Another inconsistency is that the VaR is sometimes equated with the quantile of the loss distribution and sometimes to the difference between the quantile and the expected loss. Here, the following definition is used for the VaR ρ^{VaR}:

$$\rho^{VaR}(\tilde{L}) = min\,(l : P\,(L \geq l) \leq \alpha)$$

where $\tilde{L}$ is total portfolio loss and $\alpha \in (0,1)$ is small. This risk measure is not coherent neither, since it lacks the attribute of subadditivity. Frey and McNeil (2002), p. 4, give an example for a bond portfolio with nonsensical implications when calculating VaR.

The expected shortfall or conditional Value at Risk ("ES") is a coherent risk measure and hence preferred to VaR by academics. The intention behind ES is to compute the mean of the loss distribution conditional on exceeding a certain loss threshold, which is usually defined in terms of VaR. Thus, for a small $\alpha \in (0,1)$ the risk measure ρ^{ES} of total portfolio loss L with continuous distribution is defined as:

$$\rho^{ES}(L) = \frac{1}{\alpha}\int_{1-\alpha}^{1} \rho^{VaR_{1-x}}(L)dx$$

where $\rho^{VaR_\alpha}(L)$ stands for the VaR risk measure at level α. A detailed discussion of the expected shortfall in terms of the more general concept of lower partial moments is given in Guthoff et al. (1998).

[7]For the regulatory model, see section 4.5. VaR is incorporated in the transformation of the probability of default as outlined in section 6.5.2.

5.1.3 Risk Contributions

Theoretically, market efficiencies should ensure that portfolios and sub-portfolios are efficient. In reality, however, particularly in credit risk management, the risk manager is confronted with inefficient portfolios. As pointed out in section 2.3.3, one source in car finance and lease contracts may be sale considerations in connections with the limited liquidity of the underlying contracts. Such portfolios have to be optimized in a step-by-step procedure, necessitating the repeated evaluation of individual risk contributions at each step.[8]

From this follows that, in addition to the risk measurement for the portfolio as a whole, equivalent calculations are required for each individual asset and sub-portfolio of assets. Such risk contributions $\rho_i(\tilde{L})$ must be measured consistently with the portfolio risk measure $\rho(\tilde{L})$. There are at least three additional requirements: intuition, additivity, and practicability.[9] Ad-dititivity requires that the sum of the risk contributions be equal to the portfolio risk measure: $\sum_i \rho_i(\tilde{L}) = \rho(\tilde{L})$. Practicability necessitates, for example, that the calculation of the risk contributions be possible in a fast manner. In literature, broadly five different allocation rules for the computation of risk contributions are discussed: allocation based on volumes or on local risk measures, the with/without principle, the marginal impact principle, and the allocation according to the Euler principle.[10] Apart from these general allocation principles, further schemes are available for specific models and underlying risk measures.[11]

Traditionally, capital allocation has been exclusively involved with additivity and applicablity, examples being the allocation based on **volumes** or on **local risk measures**. Assuming that the risk measure $\rho(\tilde{L})$ for the total portfolio is given, the former approach allocates capital to sub-portfolios by multiplying $\rho(\tilde{L})$ with the percentage of sub-portfolio to total volume. Under the latter approach, the multiplier is a percentage of the sub-portfolio's isolated

[8](See Kurth and Tasche, 2003, p. 84).

[9]See Koyluoglu and Stoker (2002),p. 90, or Patrik et al. (1999).

[10]Another interesting, but for large portfolios infeasible approach, is described in Koyluoglu and Stoker (2002). Using the game theory framework developed in Shapley (1953), it is possible to calculate risk contributions based on the analogy of "bribing" members to stay in a coalition.

[11]See Lehrbass et al. (2001) for a calculation scheme for VaR risk contributions in CR+. Martin et al. (2001b) describe how to derive risk contributions in CR+ using the saddlepoint approach.

risk measure to the sum of the sub-portfolios' risk measures. Both approaches guarantee that the risk contributions sum up to the portfolio risk measure. On the other hand, allocation principles based on individual risk measures neglect portfolio effects. Allocation based on volumes is, in addition, not risk adjusted.

Another approach is allocation according to the **with/without principle**, also known as decomposition into discrete marginal contributions. Under this rule, the portfolio risk measure is computed once for the overall portfolio and ceteris paribus excluding each different sub-portfolio. Then the risk contribution for each portfolio is set equal to the difference in risk measures including and excluding the portfolio. This approach is intuitive but has two chief drawbacks. First, the contributions do not generally add up to the portfolio risk measure. Thus, they are difficult to interpret both absolutely and in relation to $\rho(\tilde{L})$. Further, from a practical point of view, the computational time can increase vastly, since, for n sub-portfolios, the loss distribution has to be calculated $n+1$ times. In particular, the computation of risk contributions for each contract in a large portfolio by using a simulation model should not be feasible.

Under the **marginal impact principle** partial derivatives or approximations thereof are calculated for each sub-portfolio. Let $\rho\left(\tilde{L}(\mathbf{X})\right)$ again denote the risk measure, where $\mathbf{X} = (X_1, ..., X_n)$ are the volumes of each sub-portfolio and $\mathbf{E}_i$ is a vector of dimension n with zeros except in position i. Then for a sufficiently small $h \in \mathbb{R}$ the risk contribution based on the marginal impact principle is defined as:

$$\rho_i\left(\tilde{L}\right) = \frac{\rho\left(\tilde{L}\left(\mathbf{X} + h \cdot \mathbf{E}_i\right)\right) - \rho\left(\tilde{L}\left(\mathbf{X}\right)\right)}{h}, \qquad E_i = (0, .., 0, 1, 0, .., 0)^T$$

This allocation rule is preferable to the with/without principle, since the risk contributions should approximately add up. The difference is contingent on the quality of the linear approximation and, thus, on the form of $\rho(\tilde{L})$ and the choice of h. The latter is subjective and difficult to choose, especially in portfolios with varying volumes. In addition, the approach requires that the loss $\tilde{L}_i$ of a sub-portfolio with volume X_i can be seen as a multiple of the loss $\tilde{U}_i$ of a sub-portfolio with volume one, that is $\tilde{L}_i = X_i \cdot \tilde{U}_i$. This is closely related to the attribute of positive homogeneity of the risk measure. If this is not the case, vast changes in the risk contribution may occur for small changes in h. Finally, multiple calculations for different portfolios are required when applying the with/without principle, which might not be feasible in practice.

The last allocation approach was first suggested in Littermann (1996) and was developed formally by Haaf and Tasche (2002). It employs the **Euler relation** for differentiable, positive homogeneous functions and suggests that the risk contributions be calculated as weighted derivatives, where ν_i is the exposure with regard to asset i:

$$\rho_i\left(\tilde{L}\right) = \nu_i \cdot \frac{\partial \rho\left(\tilde{L}\right)}{\partial \nu_i}$$

Haaf and Tasche (2002) show that, when using the Euler allocation principle, the risk contributions are additive. The Euler relation is also the only allocation principle in accordance with risk adjusted return on capital ("RaRoC").[12]

5.2 Portfolio Risk Measures and Contributions in CreditRisk+

5.2.1 Portfolio Risk Measures

CR+ is a model to calculate the overall loss distribution. Based on the loss distribution, the calculation of the risk measures VaR $\rho^{VaR}(\tilde{L})$, expected shortfall $\rho^{ES}(\tilde{L})$ and standard deviation $\rho^{SD}(\tilde{L})$ is available.[13] Alternatively, for some models an analytical solution based on the portfolio inputs is available for $\rho^{SD}(\tilde{L})$, which can be used to validate the derived loss distribution. Using conditional moments and the law of iterated expectations the analytical variance of the loss distribution in the original CR+ model is available. For convenience, define $\Psi := \left(\tilde{X}^{(1)}, \tilde{X}^{(2)}, \ldots\right)$, then the variance can be computed as:[14]

$$\begin{aligned}
\left(\rho^{SD}(\tilde{L})\right)^2 &= E\left(\tilde{L}^2\right) - E^2\left(\tilde{L}\right) \\
&= E\left[E\left(\tilde{L}^2|\Psi\right)\right] - E^2\left[E\left(\tilde{L}|\Psi\right)\right] \\
&= E\left[E\left(\tilde{L}^2|\Psi\right)\right] - E\left[E^2\left(\tilde{L}|\Psi\right)\right] + E\left[E^2\left(\tilde{L}|\Psi\right)\right] - E^2\left[E\left(\tilde{L}|\Psi\right)\right] \\
&= E\left[V\left(\tilde{L}|\Psi\right)\right] + V\left[E\left(\tilde{L}|\Psi\right)\right].
\end{aligned}$$

[12]For risk-adjusted performance measures such as RaRoC, see section 6.1.2.

[13]$\rho^{VaR}(L)$ can also be computed by the saddlepoint approximation as outlined in section 4.4.1.

[14](See Lehrbass et al., 2001, p. 22).

Due to the conditional independence of the sector rates $\widetilde{X}^{(s)}$, the first term is equal to:

$$E\left[V\left(\tilde{L}|\Psi\right)\right] = E\left[\sum_{i\in I} \widetilde{X}_i \cdot \nu_i^2\right] = \sum_{i\in I} PD_i \cdot \nu_i^2$$

From the independence follows also for the second term that:

$$\begin{aligned} V\left[E\left(\tilde{L}|\Psi\right)\right] &= V\left(\sum_{i\in I} \nu_i \cdot PD_i \cdot \sum_{s\in S} \theta_i^{(s)} \cdot \widetilde{X}^{(s)}\right) \\ &= \sum_{s\in S} V\left(\sum_{i\in I} \nu_i \cdot PD_i \cdot \theta_i^{(s)} \cdot \widetilde{X}^{(s)}\right) \\ &= \sum_{s\in S}\sum_{i\in I}\sum_{j\in I} Cov\left(\nu_i \cdot PD_i \cdot \theta_i^{(s)} \cdot \widetilde{X}^{(s)}, \nu_j \cdot PD_j \cdot \theta_j^{(s)} \cdot \widetilde{X}^{(s)}\right) \\ &= \sum_{s\in S} \frac{\sigma^{(s)\,2}}{\mu^{(s)}} \sum_{i\in I} \nu_i \cdot PD_i \cdot \theta_i^{(s)} \sum_{j\in I} \nu_j \cdot PD_j \cdot \theta_j^{(s)} = \left(\rho^{SD}(L)\right)^2 \end{aligned}$$

Thus, the variance of portfolio loss is given by:

$$\begin{aligned} \left(\rho^{SD}(\tilde{L})\right)^2 &= \sum_{i\in I} PD_i \cdot \nu_i^2 + \sum_{s\in S} \frac{\sigma^{(s)\,2}}{\mu^{(s)}} \sum_{i\in I} \nu_i \cdot PD_i \cdot \theta_i^{(s)} \sum_{j\in I} \nu_j \cdot PD_j \cdot \theta_j^{(s)} \qquad (5.1) \\ &= \sum_{i\in I} PD_i \cdot \nu_i^2 + \sum_{s\in S} \frac{\sigma^{(s)\,2}}{\mu^{(s)}} \left(\epsilon^{(s)}\right)^2 \end{aligned}$$

where $\epsilon^{(s)} = \sum_{i\in \text{Sector } s} PD_i \nu_i$. For the generalized case in the model proposed in Bürgisser et al. (2001), the formulae are given in theorem 3, p. 56.[15]

5.2.2 Risk Contributions

Contributions to ρ^{SD}

According to the Euler relation principle, risk contributions to the standard deviation, can be computed by the following corollary 6. This scheme for the calculation of risk contributions has also been suggested in the original CreditRisk+ documentation.[16] Bürgisser et al. (2001), p. 22, also give the formulae for the general model with correlated default rate sectors and loss rate segments.

[15]For the slight deviations between the formulae, see Kurth and Tasche (2003), p. 84.
[16](See Wilde, 1997a, p. 53).

Corollary 6 (Lehrbass et al. (2001), p. 22) *The risk contribution $\rho_i^{SD}(\tilde{L})$ of a contract i to the portfolio standard deviation $\rho^{SD}(L)$is given by:*

$$\rho_i^{SD}\left(\tilde{L}\right) = \frac{\nu_i \cdot PD_i}{\rho^{SD}(\tilde{L})}\left(\nu_i + \sum_{s\in S}\left(\frac{\sigma^{(s)}}{\mu^{(s)}}\right)^2 \cdot \varepsilon^{(s)} \cdot \theta_i^{(s)}\right).$$

Proof. Using the standard deviation given in equation 5.2, p. 78:

$$\begin{aligned}
\rho_i^{SD}\left(\tilde{L}\right) &= \nu_i \cdot \frac{\partial \rho^{SD}(\tilde{L})}{\partial \nu_i} \qquad (5.2)\\
&= \frac{\nu_i}{2\rho^{SD}(L)} \cdot \frac{\partial\left(\rho^{SD}(\tilde{L})\right)^2}{\partial \nu_i}\\
&= \frac{\nu_i}{2\cdot\rho^{SD}(\tilde{L})} \cdot \left[\sum_{s\in S} 2\cdot\theta_i^{(s)} \cdot PD_i \cdot \varepsilon^{(s)} \cdot \left(\frac{\sigma^{(s)}}{\mu^{(s)}}\right)^2 + 2\cdot PD_i \cdot \nu_i\right]\\
&= \frac{PD_i \cdot \nu_i}{\rho^{SD}(\tilde{L})} \cdot \left[\sum_{s\in S} \theta_i^{(s)} \cdot \varepsilon^{(s)} \cdot \left(\frac{\sigma^{(s)}}{\mu^{(s)}}\right)^2 + \nu_i\right]
\end{aligned}$$

■

Contributions to ρ^{VaR} and ρ^{ES}

The computation of risk contributions to the ρ^{VaR} and ρ^{ES} according to the Euler principle is described in Kurth and Tasche (2003). Following Gouriéroux et al. (2000) and Hallerbach (2003), for instance, the authors use the result that, if the two risk measures are partially differentiable, the derivatives can be expressed as conditional expectations:

$$\begin{aligned}
\frac{\partial \rho^{VaR}(\tilde{L})}{\partial \nu_i} &= E\left[\tilde{I}_i | \tilde{L} = \rho^{VaR}(\tilde{L})\right]\\
\frac{\partial \rho^{SD}(\tilde{L})}{\partial \nu_i} &= E\left[\tilde{I}_i | \tilde{L} > \rho^{VaR}(\tilde{L})\right]
\end{aligned}$$

Here, $\tilde{I}_i$ denotes the default variable of borrower i, which is approximated by a Poisson distribution.

As Kurth and Tasche (2003), p. 88, show, the RHS can be reformulated after computing the loss distribution twice for different parameter settings. Let $P_\alpha(L = l)$ denote the probability of loss l using the original setting, where $\widetilde{X}^{(s)}$ is distributed with parameters $\alpha = E^2(\widetilde{X}^{(s)})/V(\widetilde{X}^{(s)})$ and $\beta = V(\widetilde{X}^{(s)})/E(\widetilde{X}^{(s)})$.[17] The second loss distribution can then be

[17](See Wilde, 1997a, p. 45).

calculated ceteris paribus using $\alpha + 1 = E^2(\widetilde{X}^{(s)})/V(\widetilde{X}^{(s)}) + 1$. The authors also cite references to the calculation in the case of multiple segments.[18] Employing this notation, the conditional expectations can be expressed as:[19]

$$
\begin{aligned}
E\left[\tilde{I}_i|\tilde{L} = \rho^{VaR}(\tilde{L})\right] &= PD_i \frac{P_{\alpha+1}\left(\tilde{L} = \rho^{VaR}(\tilde{L}) - \nu_i\right)}{P_\alpha\left(\tilde{L} = \rho^{VaR}(\tilde{L})\right)} \\
E\left[\tilde{I}_i|\tilde{L} > \rho^{VaR}(\tilde{L})\right] &= PD_i \frac{P_{\alpha+1}\left(\tilde{L} > \rho^{VaR}(\tilde{L}) - \nu_i\right)}{P_\alpha\left(\tilde{L} > \rho^{VaR}(\tilde{L})\right)}
\end{aligned}
$$

Lehrbass et al. (2001), p. 24, suggest an alternative scheme for VaR risk contributions motivated by the well-known normal approximation of the quantiles. The approach is based on the following reformulation of $\rho^{VaR}(\tilde{L})$ at a level α of the portfolio loss $\tilde{L}$:

$$\rho^{VaR}\left(\tilde{L}\right) = E\left(\tilde{L}\right) + \omega \cdot \rho^{SD}\left(\tilde{L}\right).$$

Since the loss distribution is given, the expected value $E(\tilde{L})$, the VaR $\rho^{VaR}(\tilde{L})$ and the standard deviation $\rho^{SD}(\tilde{L})$ can be computed. Thus, the equation can be solved for ω. Assuming that single assets have only weak impact on the quantiles of the loss distribution, the risk contributions to VaR are then approximated by employing the risk contributions $\rho_i^{SD}(\tilde{L})$:

$$\rho_i^{VaR}\left(\tilde{L}\right) = \epsilon_i + \omega \cdot \rho_i^{SD}\left(\tilde{L}\right)$$

These risk contributions add up, but by using a normal approximation neglect the specific form and the different impacts of the single contracts.

[18](See Kurth and Tasche, 2003, p. 85).

[19]The implied calculations can be simplified by using complementary probabilities: $P(\tilde{L} > l) = 1 - P(\tilde{L} \leq l)$.

Chapter 6

A Model for Securitization

This chapter contains five sections. The first section introduces the important concept of economic, as opposed to regulatory, capital ("EC"). Whereas regulatory capital is roughly equivalent to the equity held by a financial institution as required by the regulator, EC is equivalent to the "true" risk of the portfolio. EC can, for example, be measured by one of the risk measures introduced in chapter 5. As opposed to regulatory capital, EC can be used to integrate the different interest groups at a financial institution.

The following two sections analyze securitization in general and, in particular, its utilization in the automotive industry. Based on the concepts introduced by then, the fourth section develops a framework for asset-backed security ("ABS") transactions. This framework is applied to different potential motivations of an ABS issuer in form of separate optimization problems. The solutions to these problems can be interpreted as suggestions for the management of sub-optimal portfolios.

In the final section, the framework is aligned with regulatory requirements for the computation of regulatory capital as input for the models.

6.1 Capital and the Management of Financial Institutions

6.1.1 Capital

The business of financial institutions is the taking of risks. In this regard, one of the classical risks is credit risk. However, banks have different stakeholders with potentially different criteria for an optimal management of these risks.[1] A general framework which allows each party's interest to be considered within an homogenous framework is economic capital.

Capital is traditionally defined by physical assets, often separated into tiers ranging from share capital to short-term subordinated debt. In corporate finance, it has two purposes: to transfer ownership and to provide funding, where funding is possible both through issuing equity and taking on debts.[2] Return requirements of shareholders and costs of capital result in an optimal leverage. At a financial institution, however, neither this understanding of capital nor the implied mechanisms are valid any longer for two reasons. First, although as outlined in section 2.2.2 all companies bear risk as part of the business, the taking of risks is the core function of a bank. To absorb these risks, capital must be provided in addition to the funding purpose. Further, the leverage mechanisms do not necessarily work. Brealey and Myers (1996), p. 459, describe the following effect: although debt allows cheaper refinancing, rising debt levels may induce shareholders to demand higher returns on equity to compensate for the increased default risk. These mechanisms might, however, be distorted at banks due to the better access to funding, either by central banks or on the markets, and the visibility of such transactions. In particular off-balance sheet transactions can give principally unlimited leverage. An extreme example of increased leverage has been the LTCM hedgefund, which at times had a balance sheet leverage ratio of 60.[3] Although there are important differences to hedge funds, similar mechanisms can be applied at banks.

There are further reasons that call for a new capital definition and which relate to the in-

[1] In the following, the terms bank and financial institution are used synonymously.

[2] (See Matten, 2000, chap. 1).

[3] For a critical discussion of LTCM and its leverage policy see http://www.treas.gov/press/releases/reports/hedgefund.pdf.

vestment process.[4] Financial institutions have become heterogeneous and interdependencies between units have grown. Thus, businesses and units are no longer congruent, and allocating physical capital to distinct units which perform as profit centers is neither valid nor even possible. This is also true in the automotive industry, where some institutions at least strive to extend their product offerings to complexly structured products beyond loan and lease contracts.

The same considerations imply that traditional performance measures based on physical capital are no longer valid.[5] An alternative definition and purpose of capital should, in particular, include the balance between the amount of physical "idle money" kept to absorb losses and the return demands of the shareholders. As an example where purposes collide, Matten (2000), p. 18, notes that banks empirically hold an amount of physical capital well in advance of the regulatory requirements. He offers different reasons for this observation, which is seemingly at odds with shareholder demands. Reasons include the better internal evaluation of risks and the pressure applied by rating agencies.

Different and potentially conflicting views on capital are further analyzed in the next section. A unifying framework evolving around the concept of economic capital is presented.

6.1.2 Views on Capital at Financial Institutions

Matten (2000) identifies four different internal and external parties with varying purposes, capital definitions, and allocation approaches. The first is **treasury**, which is concerned with cash management, i.e. optimization of the availability and investment of physical capital. Second is the **regulator**, which is interested in a safe, sound, and fair landscape for financial institutions in general. Thus, regulators require financial institutions to hold regulatory capital, i.e. minimum physical capital. The calculation rules for regulatory capital are necessarily crude, since they must be applicable to a multitude of heterogeneous institutions.

The third group is **risk management**, which is concerned with loss avoidance and absorption. This is done by calculating risk capital, typically using more advanced methods in

[4](See Albrecht, 1999).

[5]This includes the popular Return on Equity ("RoE").

comparison to regulatory capital, resulting in differences to regulatory capital. To ensure liquidity and avoid insolvency, usually a high quantile of the loss distribution is estimated for risk capital. The choice of an appropriate probability can, for example, be directed by the historical default probability implied by the desired rating. As an example, AA-rated bonds have a historical one year default rate of 3 bp, which suggests employing the 99.997% quantile. [6] In credit risk management even higher quantiles are calculated, which is motivated among other factors by the awareness of model and parameterization risk.[7] Finally, the fourth group encompasses the bank's **shareholders**. As risk managers, they are concerned with the avoidance and absorption of losses. Furthermore, seeing the financial institution as an investment, they demand an optimally risk-adjusted performance.

To integrate the different views within a financial institution, total economic capital must be calculated first by internal risk models. Next, a minimum risk-adjusted return or hurdle rate to be reached by investments is set by management. These minimum returns, or hurdle rates, can be constructed from funding costs or opportunity costs such as weighted average costs of capital or may be based on shareholder value considerations.[8] An example of the latter is setting the required return on equity as suggested by the capital asset pricing model ("CAPM"):

$$\text{ROE} = r_f + \beta\left(r_M - r_f\right), \text{ where } \beta = \rho\frac{\sigma}{\sigma_M}$$

Here r_f denotes the risk-free rate and r_M is the return of the market portfolio. ρ stands for the correlation between market and company returns and σ and σ_M are the standard deviations of the returns of the company and the market, respectively.[9] Economic capital is then allocated across the institution with the purpose of maximizing some risk-adjusted performance measure

[6](See BIS, 1999b, p. 14).

[7]The naive approach, setting EC equal to the maximum potential loss, is not feasible for two reasons. First, for certain option portfolios, the maximum potential portfolios loss is infinite, although this is not necessarily the case for loan portfolios in the automotive industry. The second reason addresses the nature of the business. Since managing risks is what a financial institution does, the insurance against maximum loss is equivalent to transferring the core business to another institution.

[8](See Saunders, 2002, p. 152).

[9]For more information on the CAPM see Brealey and Myers (1996) or Ross et al. (2002).

("RaPM").[10] The business units allocate the economic capital further across the respective portfolios. Ex post, realized risk-adjusted returns are calculated for management evaluation and analysis of future capital allocation.

The generic term RaPM can be used for all techniques where risk-adjusted returns are calculated. Risk adjusted returns relate earnings to capital after adjusting either one or both for risk. There are mainly two reasons for the widespread use of RaPMs today.[11] First, the shareholders require the company to be directed by some risk-adjusted performance measure which allows for optimal capital allocation with respect to the shareholder value. Second, financial institutions nowadays are widespread organizations with a high number of business units, which are often organized as profit centers with different risks. This structure calls for a uniform performance measure that can be applied across divisions.[12]

In the literature, there is no unique definition of either RaPMs in general, nor of the alternative specifications.[13] Matten (2000), p. 147, distinguishes four RaPMs: return on risk-adjusted assets ("RoRaA"), risk-adjusted return on assets ("RaRoA"), return on risk-adjusted capital (" RoRaC") and risk-adjusted return on capital ("RaRoC"). These differ first with respect to the consideration of assets or capital and second with respect to the risk adjustment of the numerator or the denominator. Asset-based measures are used rarely if at all, since they are contingent on accounting rules. Banking business, however, involves substantial off-balance sheet operations. In contrast, RoRaC and RaRoC can be defined as follows:

$$\text{RaRoC} = \frac{\text{Risk-adjusted income}}{\text{Regulatory capital}}$$

$$\text{RoRaC} = \frac{\text{Adjusted income}}{\text{Economic capital}}$$

---

[10](See Matten, 2000, p. 146).

[11](See Saunders, 2002, p. 151).

[12]For the specific requirements in heterogeneous organizations, also see the critique on physical capital outlined in the previous section.

[13]As Paul Kupiec of IMF mentioned at an online PRMIA Diskussion:"Much of what I have read on the topic [of RAROC type methods] is jibberish or (intentionally?) opaque advertisements. Unfortunately, this has not stopped many noncritical readers and managers from adopting the nonsense and even extending the number of acrynonyms that are associated with it."

According to Matten (2000), p. 147, "most RaRoC models turn out on closer inspection to use the RoRaC equation". Thus, the risk-adjustment of the RaRoC denominator is usually not further specified.[14]

In this thesis, the focus is on RoRaC and Return on Equity ("ROE"), the latter being defined as:[15]

$$\text{ROE} = \frac{\text{Adjusted income}}{\text{Regulatory capital}}$$

The controlling system at DaimlerChrysler, for example, is based on the value added which can be translated into an RoE framework.[16] It uses different hurdle rates on the group level and the division level and further differentiates between industrial businesses on the one hand and financial services on the other. For financial services, a minimum rate of return before taxes of 14% is required, which can be translated into a value added by the following formula:[17]

$$\text{Value added before tax} = (\text{ROE-}14\%) \cdot \text{Average Equity}$$

The RoE at DC is defined as operating profit over average equity, where operating profits are calculated as the periodic results of operating business activities using the cost-of-sales method. The profitability of single investments is then based on its discounted value added and the net present value.[18]

Portfolio optimization by asset-backed transactions is exploited in section 6.4.5. The optimization is based on concepts introduced in this section, e.g. the minimization of regulatory capital or RoRaC maximization. Due to current usage, and despite the observation that it is not risk adjusted and thus suboptimal, RoE optimization is also modeled.

[14] For the definition of adjusted income see section 6.4.1.

[15] For discussions on how to relate RaPMs and ROE, see Saunders (2002) and Gründl and Schmeiser (2001).

[16] For more information see the DaimlerChrysler homepage, http://www.daimlerchrysler.com.

[17] In similar settings the hurdle rate is 8% for the group and 13% for industrial businesses.

[18] The discounted value added must be larger than zero. There are no fixed rules for the net present value.

6.2 Securitization

6.2.1 Introduction

Securitization is broadly defined as the process in which often illiquid assets are bundled and traded in the market, and their cash flow or economic value is redirected to support payments on the related securities.[19] Such securities where principal and interest is covered by collateral are called asset-backed securities ("ABS"). Examples of collateral are credit cards, auto loans, home equity loans, manufactured housing or student loans. Other collateral types include collateralized bond and collateralized loan obligations. The basic concept of securitization can, however, be applied to any asset. Figure 6.1 portrays how the total volume and the number of contracts of dollar-denominated ABS transactions, a whopping $439 bn in 2002, are distributed across the collateral types. As can be seen, the percentage of auto ABS volume is significantly higher than the percentage of auto ABS contracts. Overall, in volume auto ABS transactions are second only to transactions with home equity collateral.

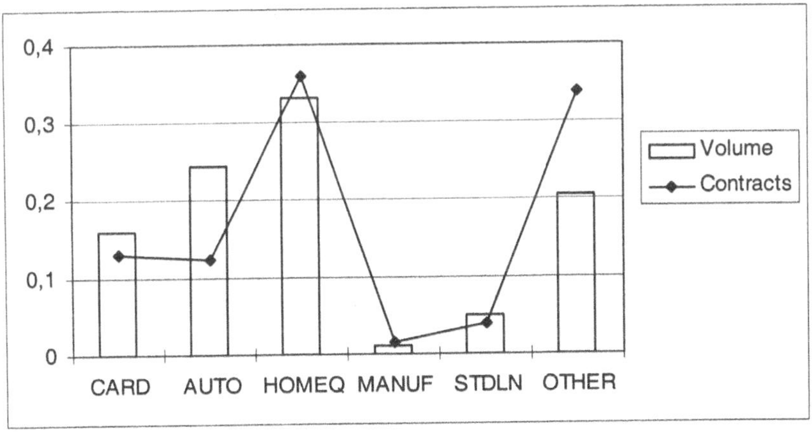

Figure 6.1: Auto Percentages of Total ABS Volume[20](Source : Bloomberg)

[19](See Bodie et al., 2002).

6.2.2 Proceedings, Classifications, and Structures of Securitization

Generally, the proceedings involved in an ABS transaction consist of different steps, which are not necessarily sequential. First, the issuer has to decide, which pool of assets is to be securitized. In particular, given recent financial innovations, the underlying asset can be constructed with extreme flexibility. Next, an underwriter that provides the necessary experience with this type of transactions is chosen. The underwriter has two tasks: to attract customers and to choose rating agencies to assign ratings to the final security. Based on the specifications, the underwriter structures a product which is marketable and is in compliance with the specifications of both the issuer and the rating agencies. This step includes a due diligence that pays special attention to the risks and risk transfers involved. Of great importance is also the writing of a detailed sale prospectus. The prospectus must thoroughly describe all the relevant issues such as the origination of the contract, the payment structure, risks and enhancements. Such enhancements may also involve external parties, e.g. in the form of a letter of credit from another bank. In the following step, the sub-portfolio is sold to a **special purpose vehicle** ("SPV") or trust. Particular importance must be paid to the examination of whether this is a **true sale**, ensuring that the SPV is "bankruptcy remote".[22] Finally, having obtained the desired ratings from one or multiple agencies, the notes on the SPV are sold to the investors. During the contract lifetime, the issuer usually provides the servicing in collaboration with the SPV. In the case of underlying loans, the borrowers are usually not even aware that their contracts have been sold. In exchange for the servicing, both the issuer and the SPV receive a fee. The structure of a typical ABS transaction with car loans as underlying assets is given in figure 6.2. In this example, the loan contracts are sold from the captive to a special purpose vehicle. By obtaining the asset-backed securities issued by the SPV the investors are entitled to principal and interest which are based on the borrower payments. Two main classifications are mentioned in

[20]CARD: Credit Card Loans, AUTO: Vehicle Loan&Lease, HOMEQ: Home Equity, MANUF: Industrial, STDLN: Student Loans

[22]The potential of ABS and credit derivatives to feign such a true sale, and thus a complete risk transfer, has also been a major critique of the old capital regime Basle I.

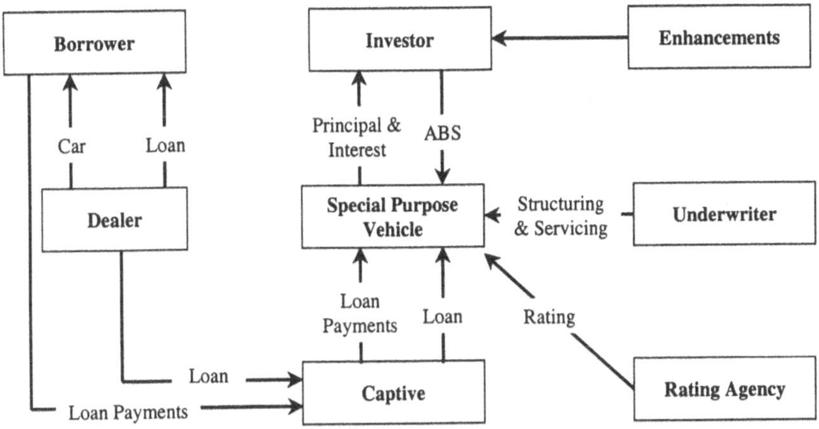

Figure 6.2: Auto ABS Structure

the literature. First, **balance sheet** and arbitrage, or **synthetic**, ABS can be differentiated.[23] For the former, the underlying assets are based on balance sheet items, which are removed from the books by the transaction. With the latter, the underlying assets are acquired with the special intention to create an ABS, often with the proceedings from selling the ABS notes. The motivation for the issuer in this case is the generation of arbitrage gains from interest differences between the ABS notes and, for example, the underlying loans. Synthetic securitizations are independent of the issuer's portfolio. For this reason, investing in such a transaction is similar to investing in a fund focusing on assets with credit risk such as bonds. An ABS can also be classified as either **pass-through** or **pay-through** transactions. In the first case, payments flow through to the holders on a pro-rata basis. In the second case, cash flows are allocated by the SPV. Whereas balance sheet ABS are invariantly pass-through transactions in nature, arbitrage ABS can be of both types.

Relevant structural elements of ABS securities are underlying assets, payment structure and enhancements. In general, any asset, in particular debt instruments, can be underlying.

[23](See Bund, 2000).

Apart from traditional collateral such as auto or housing loans, bonds, bank loans or mixtures have become popular, giving rise to collateralized bond obligations ("CBO"), collateralized loan obligations ("CLO") and collateralized debt obligations ("CDO"). Since the modeling of portfolio effects is a problem, traditionally only homogeneous and diversified portfolios or those with publicly rated securities underlying have been securitized.

With regard to the payment structure, two classifications are of relevance: payments can be separated into amortizing and non-amortizing assets and issuances. Non-amortizing assets do not pay a rate on a declining balance; the chief example are credit cards and revolving loans. Such assets allow securities with long average lives to be created on assets with short maturity. Whereas finance and lease contracts are amortizing, an important example of non-amortizing assets in the automotive industry are dealer floor-plans.

The second major classification is into payments that are equally distributed among investors, and payment structures that consist of **tranches**. The usual case are ABS transactions structured into tranches varying in coupon, seniority, maturity, and hence risk. In plain vanilla transactions, every tranche receives the same portion of the interest, but the principal is used to pay back the most senior tranches first. Tranches may also offer floating rate payments, or they are structured as strips, which only offer participation in interest or principal payments of the underlying assets.

Tranches with the lowest seniorities are often kept by the issuer which serves as an enhancement for the investor by absorbing certain losses. These tranches are also called first loss pieces ("FLP"). Other enhancements which protect investors from credit risk are given in table 6.1. They are separated into internal and external enhancements, where the latter expose the investor to third-party credit risk. Examples are guaranties, which are equivalent to letters of credit. Excess spreads are differences in interest payments between the ABS and the underlying assets. These can be channeled into a separate reserve fund to provide an additional cushion. Cash collateral amounts are employed for the same purpose. They are set up in advance by the issuer, e.g. in the form of short-term securities. These can also be sold to protect investors

Credit Risk	
External Enhancements	**Internal Enhancements**
Loss Insurance	Subordination
Third Party Guaranties	Overcollateralization
Letter of Credit	Excess Spread
	Reserve Fund
	Cash Collateral Account

Table 6.1: External and Internal ABS Enhancements

when losses increase. Enhancements can also serve to alleviate prepayment risk.[24]

Due to such enhancements, ABS transactions often obtain the highest rating AAA. However at least in volume, the issues with a lesser rating are increasing as depicted in figure 6.3. A general trend towards the securitization of riskier assets would be in accordance with the growing creditworthiness of auto loan and lease customers due to increased sales pressure.

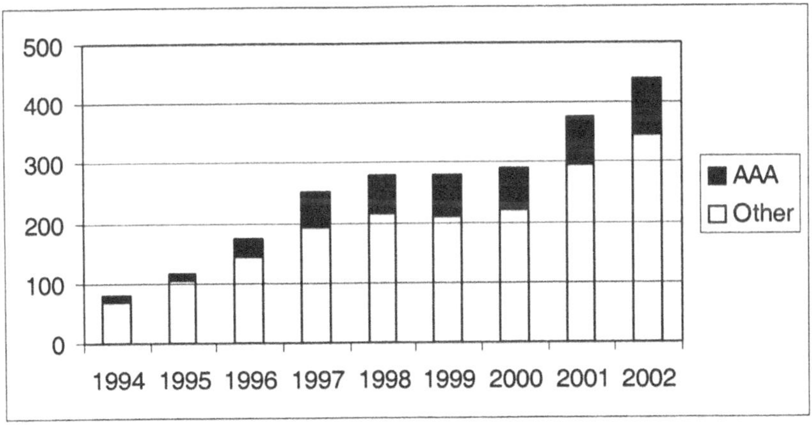

Figure 6.3: ABS Issues Rated AAA or Other, in Bio $ (Source : Bloomberg)

[24](See Karr et al., 1997, p. 76).

6.2.3 Motivation for Securitizations

Motivations for Issuers

Most motivations for securitization from an issuer's perspective can be aligned with five groups. The first group encompasses motivations that relate to **regulatory capital**. Examples are the desire to generally decrease the amount of regulatory capital. Another motivation is regulatory capital arbitrage, assuming significant deviations between regulatory and economic capital. Capital arbitrage can involve a "true sale", where assets are removed from the sheets but the issuer retains a first loss piece. Another alternative which has been used are credit derivatives such as credit swaps.[25]

The second group of motivations is based on **funding** considerations. In this regard, securitizations offer a fast and cheap alternative to traditional funding at large volumes. This assumes a proper execution and a rating of the ABS transaction which is better than that of the issuer. Additionally, this motivation allows financing from different sources, including fixed income investors, thus avoiding the dependence on single institutions.

A third line of motivations are **risk and activity efficiencies**. Risk efficiency can be increased, for instance, when the risk inherent in illiquid assets can be transferred. In contrast, finance and lease contracts were traditionally "bought and held" by banks. A transfer can help to decrease concentration risk, or to avoid the impacts of mispricing. An example of the latter are car sales campaigns which offer special customer rates and result in large, under-priced sub-portfolios. In addition, investors have better access to diversification assets. This can enable spreads to be decreased and thereby improving the conditions offered to the borrowers at the issuing institution. Activity efficiency is improved when companies are able to focus on their core competencies, e.g. producing and selling cars, instead of asset management.

The last two groups of motivations relate to **balance sheet improvement** and **transparency**. With regard to the former, it may be of interest to reduce the leverage by securitizing debt and thus obtain a better standing with the rating agencies. Another motivation is to boost liquidity quickly. Finally, securitized portfolios increase transparency, which is of special importance

[25] See Bluhm et al. (2002), p. 254 for an example of capital arbitrage under Basle I.

for the performance measurement of the shareholders.

Other motivations include the **generation of servicing fees** without increasing the capital base, and the **management of interest rate risk.**[26] The first motivation assumes that while the contracts are securitized, the services are retained. Thus, usually a financial institution can levy charges for the provision of computational or collection functions. Improved interest rate risk management is possible when payments are matched with funding. In addition, it is generally possible to separate interest and credit risk.

From a practical point of view, there are also reasons against securitization. These concern the complexity of such transactions, and the resulting personal and legal requirements. Companies might also want to take into account a potential downturn of the ABS markets. However, for the supporting reasons outlined above, the usage of securitization in the automotive industry is not likely to decrease in the future. The availability of, potentially underpriced, loans and lease contracts, banking issues such as regulatory capital, and the development of credit models should instead further promote a trend towards securitization.

Motivations for Investors

From an investor's point of view, ABS transactions offer at least three advantages. First, they usually provide a relatively high yield in comparison to other securities with the same rating. The reasons are credit enhancements, which improve the rating, and a potential "innovation spread" in the case of financial innovations.[27] Whether the latter will continue in mature markets remains to be seen. In some ABS classes, yields also increase due to prepayment risk. Second, ABS can be tailored to the investors' wishes with regard to interest, maturities, and risk. Finally, such securities allow the entry into markets which would otherwise be inaccessible or illiquid.

On the other hand, ABS transactions involve general and asset-specific types of risk. A general risk class is the credit risk of the collaterals, e.g. financial distress of a car buyer. Interest rate risk also causes price volatility for any fixed-income instruments. It is of special signifi-

[26](See Bhattacharya and Fabozzi, 1997, p. 9).

[27]See Bhattacharya and Fabozzi (1997), p. 10. Examples of enhancements are given in table 6.1.

cance for investors in ABS due to its interconnection with prepayment risk. Prepayment risk arises because ABS transactions, particularly mortgage-backed securitizations ("MBS"), allow repayment of the principal before maturity. Since this option is attractive to borrowers especially when interest rates are low, reinvestment risk arises for the ABS investors. Prepayment risk from an investor's point of view is also implied in embedded options such as bullets and early amortization rules. The former allow the issuer to buy the contract back from investors before maturity. This can be attractive when legal and other expenses needed to keep the security in the market become proportionally too high. Examples are the costs for regulatory filings. Early amortization, in contrast, serves to protect investors from credit risk. Given that the underlying portfolio is in distress, the assets can be distributed to the investors to protect them from a further deterioration. The reduction of credit risk, however, is counteracted by the implied increase in prepayment risk.

Generally, interest rate risk is lower for structures paying floating rates. Prepayment risk is also of less importance for non-mortgage ABS transactions. This is due to the relatively short maturity and generally lower interest rates involved in such transactions. Especially auto contracts based, for example, on promotional prices can be expected to be relatively immune. However, tranched ABS transactions are highly complex, and the required level of legal and financial analysis usually restricts them to institutional investors. Of these, due to their investment strategy, pension funds prefer ABS tranches with high ratings and stable cash flows. In contrast, insurance companies are more yield oriented and may prefer to invest in subordinated tranches.

Economic Impacts of Securitization

The economic impacts of securitization can be both positive and negative.[28] Among the positive effects are, first, decreasing costs of financial intermediation, given a matured, and perhaps a standardized, securitization process. Such impacts include also efficiencies with regard to scale effects, allocation, and information. Economies of scale can be realized when funding is

[28](See Bhattacharya and Fabozzi, 1997).

increased by securitization, and the advances employed to generate additional business. Second, allocation efficiency is improved since contracts become fungible and must no longer be held until maturity. This effect includes better market access for niche companies.

Additional positive impacts relate to information efficiencies and specific underlying assets supported by the government. Information efficiency is, for example, improved when appropriate customer rates are induced by backward induction from market prices. Economic advantages can also be realized when the assets underlying an ABS transaction are supported by the government. Examples in the US are student loans and mortgages. MBS transactions, in particular, are distributed by governmental organizations such as the governmental national mortgage association, the federal national mortgage association or the federal home loan mortgage corporation.

On the other hand, there are at least four potential negative impacts of securitization. First, securitization can make adverse selection attractive. Given that bad risks require more enhancements to make the security sellable in the market, yet yield higher interest, a financial institution might be tempted to securitize good risks only. As a counter argument, at least for transparent risks, this should be reflected in decreasing company ratings. A similar argument suggests that it should also not be possible to securitize exclusively bad risks due to the transaction rating, the due diligence process, and the reputation risk involved. A final critique concerns regulatory capital arbitrage, particularly in the case of securities where the monies are not passed through. In this case the risk is not transferred completely, but regulatory loopholes may permit that capital not be adjusted accordingly.

6.2.4 Excursion: Moody's Approach to Asset-backed Securities

The rating agencies play a crucial role in the success of a securitization transaction. In such transactions, particularly due to the complexity of the underlying structure, the investors have to rely on the published ratings. Especially Moody's has been able to outline its quantitative approaches in a reasonably transparent way which is also considered in academia.[29]

[29](See Bluhm et al., 2002, p. 271).

Moody's has suggested two models especially suitable for ABS transactions, which use the lognormal distribution and the (double) binomial expansion ("BET"). Regarding classical ABS transactions, the BET is employed for collateralized debt obligations and commercial mortgage-backed securitizations, whereas the lognormal approach is taken especially for granular ABS transactions and residential mortgage-backed securitizations. To generalize, if underlying are a small number of homogeneous assets, the BET should be used and, in case of a large number of homogeneous assets, the lognormal distribution.[30]

An approach employing Fourier transformations ("FTM") has only recently been developed to encounter the growing trend to securitize heterogeneous pools in terms of credit risk, size or maturity. As the first two approaches, it avoids Monte Carlo simulation techniques. Moody's uses simulation techniques, however, for transactions which contain market-driven underlying assets. An outline and references are given in Debuysscher and Szego (2003), p. 2.

In the case of automotive ABS usually relatively homogeneous assets are underlying. This is especially true for the securitization of retail portfolios, suggesting that, for car securitization, either the BET or the lognormal approach be used. As, in addition, it is "not Moody's intention to replace its existing methodologies with the FTM", FTM and simulation approaches are not further outlined. However, all approaches represent mixtures of art and science, the former becoming obvious, for example, in the parameterization and the cash flow modeling. Moody's is well aware of this and of the limits of quantitative modeling, as is obvious from the following quote: "Ultimately, there is no viable way to eliminate the human component of ABS analysis without sacrificing robustness".[31]

The (Double) Binomial Expansion Technique

The BET is based on the derivation of a diversity score. The diversity score is the number of uncorrelated and homogeneous loans or bonds in a hypothetical portfolio with the same risk profile.[32] All these loans or bonds are identical in par value and probability p, which under

[30](See Debuysscher and Szego, 2003, p. 1).

[31](See Ernst, 2001, p. 1).

[32]For the BET see Cifuentes and O'Connor (1996).

the assumption of independence implies the binomial distribution for total losses. The rating approach consists of four steps: the derivation of the standardized parameters, the computation of the diversity score, the evaluation of the expected loss per tranche, and the final assignment of the rating.

The homogeneous default probability p and the loss rate are derived as weighted averages, usually based on historical realizations.[33] Parameters may additionally be adjusted by stressing factors.[34] There are different alternatives for deriving the most important input, which is the diversity score D. Their respective applicability depends on the data availability. Especially in the case of bonds, default correlations $\rho_{i,j}$ may be available between assets i and j. In this case, the following formula, which can be significantly simplified for homogeneous portfolios, can be applied:[35]

$$D = \frac{(\sum_i PD_i F_i)(\sum_i q_i F_i)}{\sum_i \sum_j \sqrt{PD_i PD_j q_i q_j F_i F_j}}$$

Here F_i denotes the face value of asset i, and $q_i = 1 - PD_i$.

Should correlations not be available, diversity scores can be obtained by assigning assets to one of 33 industry classes and analyzing the number of assets per industry using an ad hoc rule. In this case, Moody's applies the information in table 6.2.[36] If, for example, a portfolio consists of ten assets in three sectors in groups of 2, 3 and 5, the portfolio's total diversity score is equal to the sum of individual diversity scores. Using the information from the table, $D = 1.5 + 2.0 + 2.67 = 6.17$. For more than 10 instruments in one industry group, the diversity score is determined on a case-by-case basis. Since a high diversity score implies a high number of assets in the homogeneous comparison portfolio, high industry concentration lead to high diversity scores. Although Gluck and Remeza (2000), p. 1, explicitly mention the rating of collateralized loan obligations, the derivation of the diversity score for such transactions is not outlined. Instead the focus is set on bond portfolios only.

In the next step, the diversity score D and the homogeneous probability of default p are

[33](See Bluhm et al., 2002, p. 272).

[34](See Gluck and Remeza, 2000, p. 2).

[35](See Gluck and Remeza, 2000, p. 15).

[36](See Bluhm et al., 2002, p. 273).

Number of Assets in Same Industry	Diversity Score
1	1.00
2	1.50
3	2.00
4	2.33
5	2.67
6	3.00
7	3.25
8	3.50
9	3.75
10	4.00

Table 6.2: Moody's Diversity Score (Source : Bluhm et al. (2002))

used as parameters in the binomial distribution on which the number of defaults is based:

$$P\,(\text{Defaults} = d) = \frac{D!}{d!(D-d)!}p^d(1-p)^{D-d}$$

The double binomial expansion technique is a straightforward generalization of this approach. It assumes that the portfolio can be replicated by two assuming two independent homogeneous comparison portfolio.[37] In the next step, scenarios are generated as pairs of defaults in the first and the second portfolio. Thus, if D_1 and D_2 and as p_1 and p_2 describe the parameters of the two portfolios respectively, the total number of defaults have the following distribution:

$$\begin{aligned} P\,(\text{Defaults}_1 = d_1, \text{Defaults}_2 = d_2) &= \frac{D_1!}{d_1!(D_1-d_1)!}p_1^{d_1}(1-p_1)^{D_1-d_1} \cdot \\ & \quad \frac{D_2!}{d_2!(D_2-d_2)!}p_2^{d_2}(1-p_2)^{D_2-d_2} \end{aligned}$$

The double binomial expansion technique can also be extended to the case of more than two independent homogeneous comparison portfolios.

[37](See Cifuentes and Wilcox, 1998).

Using additional default timing assumptions, the present value of cash flows as implied by each number of defaults can be derived.[38] In each case, the loss is given by the difference between the present value of the cash flows and the nominal value of the assets. Total losses are then used to derive the losses for each tranche, taking into account the different seniorities. Combining the probability and the losses incurred for each tranche allows the estimation of the expected losses. These expected losses are then assigned a rating based on Moody's idealized historical data. Additional modeling complexities arise in cases of reinvestments, management fees or different payment priorities.

The Lognormal Distribution Approach

The lognormal approach also necessitates a cash flow analysis as outlined above. In contrast to the BET, no hypothetical portfolio is constructed, instead it is assumed that the cumulative default rate follows a lognormal distribution.[39] The parameters of this distribution are estimated based on an historical sample. In the next step, discrete probabilities are calculated by computing the integrals of the density function over disjunct intervals. To derive the expected loss, the discrete probabilities are assigned the corresponding losses from the cash flow analysis for each interval. Based on the expected loss and the seniority of a tranche, the rating is then assigned. Moody's analysis also involves a sensitivity analysis and the consideration of qualitative aspects, such as data quality. A simple example is introduced in Mazataud and Yomtov (2000), pp. 3.

Conclusion

Although less transparent, other rating agencies such as Standards & Poor's and Fitch use similar concepts. Rating agency models, however, cannot be employed in the context of this thesis for two reasons. First, the agencies focus on expected losses, neglecting the unexpected losses required for both regulatory and economic capital. Additionally, Bluhm et al. (2002),

---

[38] See Gluck and Remeza (2000) for a simple calculation example.

[39] See Mazataud and Yomtov (2000). In a footnote it is remarked that in some cases the net loss, instead of the cumulative default rate, follows a lognormal distribution. This case is, however, not further discussed.

p. 278, show that "the BET significantly underestimates the tail probabilities of the original portfolio". Second, there is no consideration of individual risk contributions. Yet these are crucial in the context of this thesis, which analyzes the choice of individual contracts for asset-backed securitization transactions. Apart from these two reasons, the modeling seems to evolve around a mixture of science and art, the latter becoming obvious, for example, in the choice of the default timing. For these reasons, the application of rating agencies' models in this thesis has not been feasible.

6.3 Securitization in the Automotive Industry

6.3.1 Issuer's View

Car manufacturers traditionally utilize securitization as a funding alternative, offering the advantages described below.[40] The funding goal is particular for non-banks, for whom refinancing is more costly. But as banking practices are introduced more and more into car financing, it can be expected that other motivations will also play a more important role in the decisions rendered on securitization in the future. Since captive financial institutions also serve as a sales channel, there should always be potential for the securitization, especially of mispriced, loans or leases. Nowadays, auto ABS transactions have come to play an important role. If not in contract number, auto ABS have increased in volume as can be seen from figure 6.4. In such transactions, the original finance and lease contracts, for example, are sold by the dealer to the financial service, which transfers them as part of a sub-portfolio to the SPV. Thus, interest and principal are directed from the customer to the SPV, which channels them to the investors.

6.3.2 Investors's View

Due to the complexity of ABS transactions, investors rely on the ratings provided by rating agencies. All of the three big rating agencies, Fitch, Moody's and Standard & Poor's, have published information on how they approach the rating of auto loan and lease securitization

[40](See Cantwell, 1993, pp. 55).

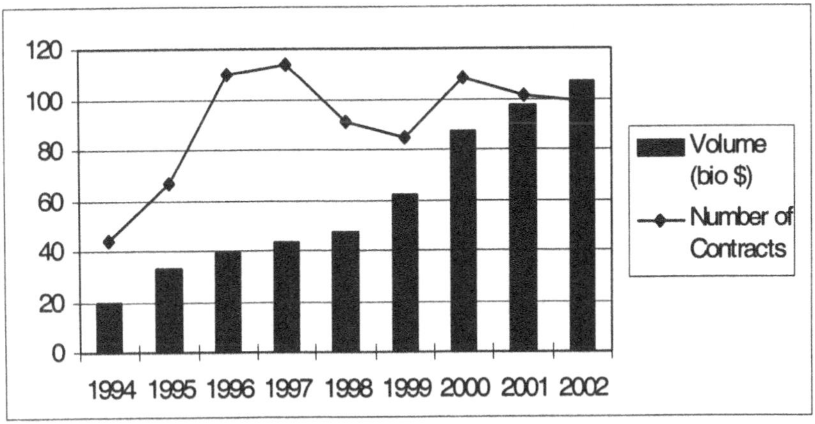

Figure 6.4: Volume and Contract Numbers of Auto ABS Issues 1994 - 2002 (Source : Bloomberg)

transactions. [41] Loan and lease transactions are usually considered separately.[42] Generally, the task of an agency is to ex ante evaluate the credit quality of a security and to monitor it over the lifetime of a contract. In the case of an ABS, the analysis should consider the seller, the particular pool, and the transaction structure, including the credit enhancements. Seller analysis includes operational reviews and a credit analysis, for instance, whereas structural analysis involves, among other things, cash flow analysis, legal aspects, and interest rate risk. Examples for credit enhancements have been given in previous chapters. The analysis of the underlying assets involves different degrees of the quantitative model, but focuses on practical applicability. The latter depends strongly on the availability of historical and/or forecast data, which are generally a problem in credit risk modeling.[43] For a critical general discussion of the

[41] See Fitch Ratings (2002), Fitch Ratings (2000), Standard&Poor's Ratings (1999), Fabrikant et al. (1995) and Dill et al. (1998).

[42] The main additional problem in lease contracts is the transfer of ownership of the vehicle, which is not considered an financial asset, see Fitch Ratings (2000), p. 4.

[43] The quantitative analysis is usually independent of the underlying pool. Moody's approaches are outlined further in section 6.2.4.

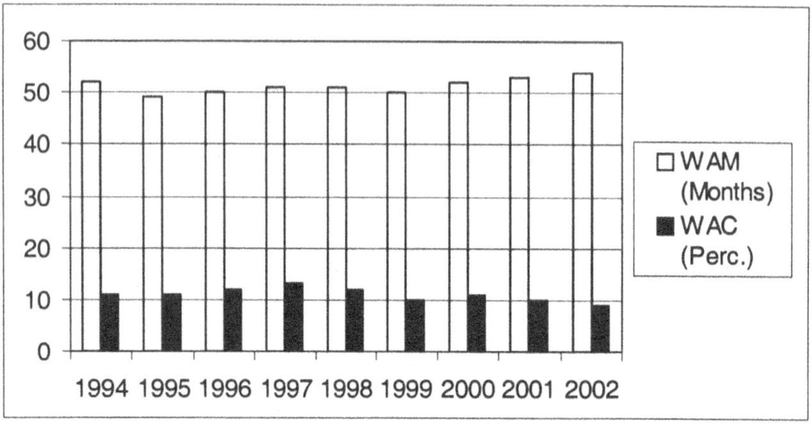

Figure 6.5: Weighted Average Maturity WAM and Weighted Average Coupon WAC of Auto ABS 1994 - 2002 (Source : Bloomberg)

rating agencies' approaches see Tavakoli (2003), p. 123.

In addition to the rating, investors rely only on a few other transaction specifics tailored to their individual investment strategy. These include the weighted average maturities and weighted average coupons, where the balances of the underlying contracts are used as weights.[44] Table 6.5 denotes the average values for dollar-nominated auto ABS in the years 1994 to 2004. These are relatively constant around 50 months and 11%. In combination with the good rating, the relatively short maturities, as a result of the average loan and lease maturities found in car financing make auto ABS attractive for institutional investors, for example.[45]

6.3.3 Securitization Example: DC Auto Trust 2002-C

The DC Auto Trust 2002-C was the third such transaction initiated by DaimlerChrysler Services North America ("DCS") in 2002.[46] It was at the same time the name of the special

[44] See Bluhm et al. (2002), pp. 66, for an example of how investors can use these measures.

[45] (See Dentz, 2003, p. 100).

[46] All information in the following are taken from the deal prospectus, available at http://www.absnet.net.

purpose vehicle to which DCS sold a pool of 125,308 automobile loans granted with a principle balance of $2.2 billion. The trustee of this vehicle in charge of distributing principal and interest was Chase Manhattan. Involved in the structuring and selling process were Credit Suisse First Boston, JP Morgan, Salomon Smith Barney, Deutsche Bank, Morgan Stanley, and Bear, Stearns & Company. The subordinated certificates, i.e. the first loss piece, as well as the rights to overcollateralization and residual cash flows were assigned to DC Retail Receivables LLC, a wholly-owned subsidiary of DCS. Further information regarding the underlying cars, geographic distribution of the contracts, selection criteria and credit experience had been provided. In this case, the contracts were chosen based on attributes relating to their individual credit quality and payment structure. For example, loans had to be less than 30 days past due for and a minimum initial balance of $ 1000.

The pool was structured into five securities with a total initial principal balance of $ 2.07 billion. Key figures regarding the tranches are set out in table 6.3. For tranche A-1, no underwriting fees are available as these were purchased by DCS to be sold afterwards. This deal contained further credit enhancements in addition to the overcollateralization implied by the difference in principal balance between the pool and the assets. The first was the certificates which were held by DCS and which served as first loss piece. In addition, from the sales proceeds DCS set up a reserve fund of $ 5.2 million to be invested in "high quality, short term investments which mature on or prior to each monthly payment date". This pool was to be utilized to reimburse both interest and principal losses due to credit losses; if possible and necessary, it was to be refilled by the collections from excess interest. These included all payments and costs which were not directly redirected to the ABS holders such as income from the reserve fund investment but also servicing fees.

The DC Auto Trust 2002-C is representative of the type of ABS issued, for example, by DaimlerChrysler and Honda. There are, however, different approaches, targeting other investor groups. An example is Ford Credit, which aims at the needs of short-term investors or offers tranches with flexible interest. Transactions such as the Ford Credit Auto Owner Trust 2003-B thus include ten tranches.

Tranche	Principal Amount	Interest Rate pa	Underwriting Fee
A-1	$ 380 m	1.79 %	N/A
A-2	$ 700 m	2.07 %	0.165
A-3	$ 550 m	2.56 %	0.188
A-4	$ 372 m	3.09 %	0.250
Certificates	$ 67 m	0.00 %	N/A

Table 6.3: Tranches of DC Auto Trust 2002-C

6.3.4 Employment of Credit Derivatives

Credit derivatives can be defined as "a specific class of financial instruments whose value is derived from an underlying market instrument driven primarily by the credit risk of either private or government entities".[47] By isolating the credit risk of an asset, they allow it to be replicated, transferred and hedged.[48] Credit derivatives pose an alternative means for credit risk transfer and are extensively used for two reasons: capital arbitrage and optimization of the risk-return profile. Credit derivatives allow one party, the protection buyer, to transfer the credit risk of an asset to one or more other parties, the protection sellers. The protection buyer, however, needs not own this asset.

Generally, three types of credit derivatives are differentiated beyond traditional financial guarantees: total-return swaps, credit default swaps, or credit-spread products, and credit-linked notes, or credit default products.[49] **Total-return swaps** are exchanges of the total return of one credit asset against that of another which may or may not contain credit risk. The total return on both assets, however, can be affected by various factors such as interest or exchange rates movements. Second, **credit default swaps** are similar in character to financial guarantees. In exchange for an upfront fee, the protection seller agrees to compensate the protection buyer upon the happening of a credit event. There is a difference to financial guarantees since credit

[47](See Ong, 1999, p. 27).

[48](See Das, 1998).

[49](See Ong, 1999).

events beyond default, e.g. downgrades, can also be transferred. In contrast to total-return swaps, however, credit default swaps only account for credit risks.

Credit-linked notes are securitized credit derivatives. The protection buyer issues notes to investors which may suffer losses in interest or principal as well as late payments, given the occurrence of specified credit events. Credit linked notes do not require a true sale as classical securitizations. As an example, the SPV issuing the notes may be the holder of a credit default swap with the original protection buyer.

Investors in credit default swaps and credit linked notes are oftentimes speculators or arbitrageurs. These groups strive to hedge their exposure, which makes it difficult to invest in assets where no replicating instruments are available. This is the case, for example, for retail loan portfolios. Thus, risk transfer and funding of automotive loan and leases traditionally relies on securitizations. These appeal to a different kind of investor, who seeks to diversify and earn the relatively high spreads. Due to their limited application, credit derivatives as alternative means of risk transfer are not further analyzed in this thesis.

6.4 A Model for the Securitization of Car Financing Contracts

6.4.1 General Setting

The research topic of this thesis is the determination of optimal sub-portfolios for securitization from an issuers point of view. This is a problem of significant practical relevance in the case that the sub-portfolio to be securitized is not prescribed by external settings, such as marketing events. To model the issuer's motivations for securitization, it is assumed that the asset-backed security consists of tranches and a first loss piece. The tranches are not further differentiated since it is assumed that the issuer holds the first loss pieces only. The generalized securitization structure is given in figure 6.6.

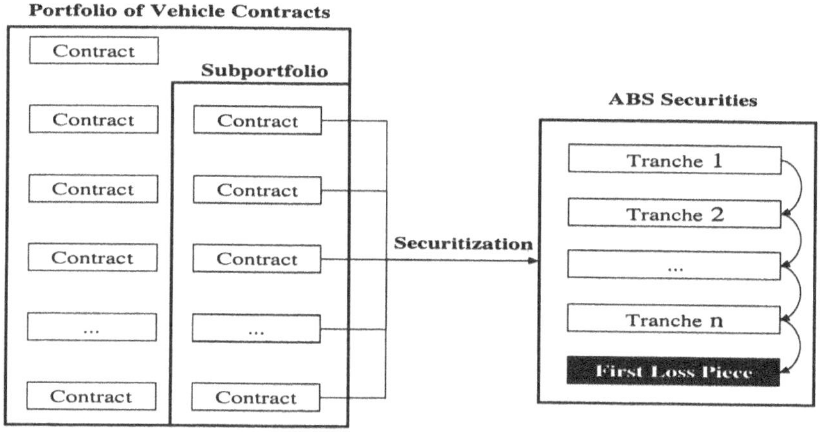

Figure 6.6: Model of Securitization Structure

For the overall portfolio, a matrix with the relevant credit information must be derived as set out in table 6.4. The calculation of the three key risk parameters exposure at default EAD, probability of default PD and loss given default LGD is assumed to be aligned with the Basle

II framework.[50] It is assumed that the true risk can only be measured by the internal model, whereas the regulatory approach is standardized, neglecting, in particular, dependencies and loss rate volatilities within the portfolio.[51] The risk contributions and the required regulatory capital are computed by the internal and the regulatory model. To ensure comparability with regulatory capital requirements, calculations of economic capital are done on a yearly basis.[52]

For the definition of adjusted income N, Ong (1999), p. 148, suggests the following generic definition:[53]

$$\text{Adjusted Income} = \text{Revenues} + / - \text{Transfer Prices} - \text{Expenses} - \text{Expected Losses}$$

It is important to distinguish adjusted income from the exposure at default EAD. The definition of EAD employed by the Basle Committee is "the amount legally owed to the bank [in the case of default]".[54] Thus, when regarding the transfer price and the expenses component, N is a more comprehensive concept with respect to the return of a transaction. The LGD parameter mitigates this effect only partly, since it considers factors influencing the economic loss *only* in the case of default. As an example, overhead for re-collection management are conditional on the default and are considered in the LGD. Overhead for the sales department, in contrast, are not, but should be factored in the expenses component of N.

Two decision variables have to be defined. First, for each contract $i \in P$ let x_i denote a binary variable. If $x_i = 1$, the contract belongs to the securitized sub-portfolio, else $x_i = 0$, although for optimization purposes, it is preferable to relax the assumption and let $x_i \in [0, 1]$. In this case, thresholds must be defined for the assignment of contracts to the securitization.

The second decision variable is the first loss piece F. Throughout the problem definitions it is assumed that the first loss piece is restricted. This restriction is applied to avoid the extreme

---

[50] See section 6.5.

[51] Matten (2000), p. 146, notes that "the main distinction between the ... [internal] model and the regulatory model is in a more precise, differentiated use of statistics...".

[52] Economic capital in CR+, for example, can also be calculated for random intervals after adjusting the input parameters, see Wilde (1997a), p. 39.

[53] For alternative definitions of adjusted income see Matten (2000), Bluhm et al. (2002) or Saunders (2002).

[54] (See BIS, 2003, §277).

Contract	Regulatory Capital	Economic Capital	Exposure at Default	Adjusted Income	Other Risk Measures
1	R_1	C_1	EAD_1	N_1	PD_1, LGD_1
2	R_2	C_2	EAD_2	N_2	PD_2, LGD_2
...	...	...	...	...	...
n	R_n	C_n	EAD_n	N_n	PD_n, LGD_n

Table 6.4: Model Inputs

case of $F = \sum_i EAD_i x_i$, which would render the securitization moot regarding both economic and regulatory capital. Since the absolute value of the relative first loss piece might be misleading, the ratio of F to the exposure of the securitization is restricted by side constraints. Examples for the sizes of first loss piece ratio in real transactions are given in table 7.1, p. 126.

Capital Requirements before and after Securitization

Regulatory and economic capital are treated separately for the securitized and the unsecuritized portion of the portfolio. Regarding the calculation of economic capital, i.e. the portfolio risk measure, after securitization, note that formally a new random variable $\widetilde{L}*$ for the loss after securitization must be defined as follows, where $\widetilde{L}_i$ denotes the loss on contract i adjusted for the securitization:

$$\widetilde{L}* = \sum_{P \setminus S} \widetilde{L}_i + \min \left\{ F, \sum_{S} \widetilde{L}_i \right\}$$

Here, P denotes the portfolio set, and S is the subset of securitized contracts. $\widetilde{L}*$ consists of two components referring to the losses from the unsecuritized and from the securitized portion of the portfolio. The losses resulting from holding the first loss piece in the securitized subportfolio, however, have an upper limit of F: $\sum_S \widetilde{L}_i \leq F$. The function $\min\{exp_1, exp_2\}$ is defined as:

$$\min\{exp_1, exp_2\} = \begin{cases} exp_1, & exp_1 \leq exp_2 \\ exp_2, & exp_1 > exp_2 \end{cases}$$

	Regulatory Capital	Economic Capital
Securitized Portfolio	$\min\{F, \sum_S R_i\}$	$\min\{F, \sum_S C_i\}$
Unsecuritized Portfolio	$\sum_{P\setminus S} R_i$	$\sum_{P\setminus S} C_i$

Table 6.5: Computation of Regulatory and Economic Capital

The distribution of $\widetilde{L}*$ for a given sub-portfolio $S \subset P$ can only be computed by simulation.[55] Thus, there is no analytical solution for neither economic capital, nor for the risk contributions. The problems involved in the employment of alternative approximations for risk contributions, such as the with/without principle, have been discussed in section 5.1.3. In addition, the distribution of $\widetilde{L}*$, and hence the economic capital as well as the risk contributions, changes with each choice of S. In this thesis, an alternative approach is chosen by at first neglecting the distribution of $\widetilde{L}*$. Instead, the portfolio risk measure is approximated directly by employing the additive risk contributions before securitization. To incorporate the upper limit imposed by the loss piece, however, the following formula is used:

$$\rho* = \sum_{P\setminus S} C_i + \min\left\{F, \sum_S C_i\right\}$$

Here $\rho*$ denotes the approximation for the economic capital after securitization. As $\widetilde{L}*$ it consists of two components for the unsecuritized and the securitized portion of the portfolio. The approximation by $\rho*$ is in analogy to the approach in setting regulatory capital requirements for securitizations. This is also based on the contributions, i.e. the regulatory capital requirements for each asset, *before* securitization: [56]

$$\rho^{Reg} = \sum_{P\setminus S} R_i + \min\left\{F, \sum_S R_i\right\}$$

The resulting formulae for economic and regulatory capital are given in table 6.5.

Using this approximation, it is possible to optimize the objectives to be introduced in the next sections. For validation, a single simulation is sufficient to derive the loss distribution for

[55](See for example Bluhm et al., 2002, p. 257).

[56]See section 6.5, equation 6.1, for the second component.

the optimized portfolio decomposition into securitized and unsecuritized contracts. Employing the loss distribution to derive economic capital allows a check to be made as to whether the objective functions have indeed been optimized.

6.4.2 Short Survey of Objectives

The purpose of this thesis is to derive an optimization framework for the securitization of sub-portfolios. The following sections suggest different modes, based on varying portfolio management strategies in the context of the general setting outlined above. In addition to the implied general strategy, the models also differ with respect to the data requirements and, thus, their respective applicability. Data availability is limited, in particular information regarding adjusted income, which is a necessary input for return calculation and optimization.

The first, basic objective modeled is to find the securitization portfolio which, given the side constraints, **minimizes regulatory capital** requirements.[57] This objective is straightforward and of special interest when equity generally is a scarce resource throughout the group. Detailed information is set out in section 6.4.3. **Regulatory capital arbitrage** goes one step further by manipulating regulatory *relative to* economic capital. This can be interpreted as the attempt to decrease equity relatively stronger than risk. As objective function, both the difference and the ratio of economic and regulatory capital can be used. The choice between these two hinges on the internal organization at the captive financial organization. When equity it to be allocated among different financial units, the difference should not be employed. Instead, the ratio can be interpreted as an investment index, which enables a comparison of the efficiency of the scarce resource equity across the different units.[58] Regulatory capital arbitrage is modeled in depth in section 6.4.4.

Economic capital measures risk, hence it can also serve as a proxy for the implied returns: if risk is considered in the borrower conditions, higher risk should imply higher interest in the underlying contracts. If such information is available, e.g. in the form of adjusted income, the

[57]The terms regulatory capital and equity are employed interchangeably in the following.

[58]From senior management's point of view, this interpretation is only feasible when there are no risk dependencies between the units. Otherwise, one unit's action also influences the economic capital of the other units.

framework can easily be applied to the explicit **optimization of traditional and risk-adjusted return measures**. The corresponding optimization problem is detailed in section 6.4.5.

The choice of a particular objective function can result in different implied securitization portfolios. Thus, it is important to decide on the objective which is feasible, given the data situation, and which can be aligned with both the group objectives and the captive's organization. A third criterion comprises political implications and the communication of the goals. Few institutions, for example, openly declare that they are or were involved in regulatory capital arbitrage. From a purely financial point of view, the optimization of risk-adjusted returns is certainly preferable. On the other hand, as has been discussed in 6.1.2, the return on equity is still a very popular measure. From these considerations follows that it is not possible to give a general recommendation.

6.4.3 Objective 1: Minimizing Regulatory Capital

Regulatory capital, i.e. equity, is a scarce resource. Car manufacturers want to keep the equity level low for two reasons. First, the captive depends on the conglomerate and defaults if and only if the conglomerate defaults. In addition, risk in automotive contracts is reduced by the vehicle as collateral. Thus, resources in general should be primarily allocated at the group level and not employed as "idle money" at the captive. This contrasts with independent financial institutions, which often hold capital above the minimum required levels to ensure against default.

The necessity to countermeasure risk by accumulating equity may be further decreased by another factor: depository insurance, which is relevant for an increasing number of captives providing additional financial services. Deposit insurance of banks ensures that a certain percentage is paid back to the depositors in the worst case. It is the prevailing view that when premiums are independent of the underlying risks, banks have incentives to increase risk levels.[59] In Germany, the DaimlerChrysler Bank, for example, offers deposits and is a member of the "Einlagensicherungsfonds" (Deposit Protection Fund of the Association of German Banks).

[59] (See John et al., 1991).

These observations suggest that ABS transactions can be employed to decrease the overall level of regulatory capital. In this first problem, the true risk as implied by the economic capital is not considered:

$$\begin{cases} & \min\{F, \sum_i R_i x_i\} + \sum_i R_i \cdot (1 - x_i) \to \min_{x_i, F} \\ s.t. & \frac{F}{\sum_i EAD_i x_i} \in [f_0, f_1] \\ & x_i \in [0, 1] \end{cases}$$

To solve the problem, the first loss piece interval $[f_0, f_1]$ must be specified in advance. Examples for empirical first loss piece sizes of DaimlerChrysler ABS are set out in table 7.1, p. 126.

6.4.4 Objective 2: Regulatory Capital Arbitrage

Matten (2000) defines regulatory capital arbitrage as "the process whereby a financial institution reduces its regulatory capital requirement with little or no corresponding reduction in its overall level of risk".[60] In the context of loan portfolios, the purpose of regulatory capital arbitrage is to hold contracts with a high level of risk, implying high interest at low levels of regulatory capital. When the economy is not in a downturn, this ensures a high return on the invested capital.

It is accepted that regulatory capital arbitrage is widespread under the old capital regime Basle I, although specific information is restricted for obvious reasons. When the Federal Reserve examined non-mortgage related ABS and asset-backed commercial paper transactions sponsored by the ten largest US bank holding companies, it came to the conclusion that "these securitization activities tend to be motivated heavily by capital arbitrage considerations".[61] Systemic forces driving regulatory capital arbitrage are analyzed, for instance, in Mingo (2000). Arbitrage may be especially attractive for institutions which use depository financing under federal or shared deposit insurance. Although the avoidance of this type of arbitrage is an explicit goal of the new regimen Basle II, the question remains as to what degree any standardized

[60](See Matten, 2000, p. 123).

[61](See BIS, 1999a, p. 25).

regulatory approach is capable of achieving this purpose.

Regulatory capital arbitrage can be modeled using different objective functions. First, one can strive to generally minimize the difference between regulatory and economic capital which can be expressed as:

$$\begin{aligned}\text{Regulatory} - \text{Economic Capital} &= \min\Big\{F, \sum_i R_i x_i\Big\} + \sum_i R_i\,(1 - x_i) \\ &\quad - \min\Big\{F, \sum\nolimits_i C_i x_i\Big\} - \sum_i C_i\,(1 - x_i) \\ &= \min\Big\{F, \sum_i R_i x_i\Big\} - \min\Big\{F, \sum\nolimits_i C_i x_i\Big\} \\ &\quad + \sum_i (R_i - C_i) \cdot (1 - x_i)\end{aligned}$$

For the optimization problem, it is again assumed that the first loss piece interval $[f_0, f_1]$ has been specified in accordance with individual requirements:

$$\begin{cases} \min\{F, \sum_i R_i x_i\} - \min\{F, \sum_i C_i x_i\} + \sum_i (R_i - C_i) \cdot (1 - x_i) \to \min\limits_{x_i, F} \\ s.t. \quad \frac{F}{\sum_i EAD_i x_i} \in [f_0, f_1] \\ \qquad x_i \in [0, 1] \end{cases}$$

A second approach is suggested if regulatory capital is a limited resource and must be allocated among other activities as well. Examples at automotive captives are hedging transactions involving market risks such as interest rate swaps. To compare the relative benefit of inducing regulatory capital for the loan and lease portfolio, the concept of a profitability index can be used.[62] Traditionally, the profitability index for an investment is defined as the ratio of the net present value of an investment to the initial investment. Different investment opportunities and limited resources given, ordering by such an index allows to determine the investment providing the largest gain per monetary unit.

To transfer the concept between regulatory capital arbitrage, the difference of economic and regulatory capital should be maximized in relation to regulatory capital as initial outlay:

$$\frac{\text{Economic} - \text{Regulatory Capital}}{\text{Regulatory Capital}} = \frac{\text{Economic Capital}}{\text{Regulatory Capital}} - 1$$

[62](See Brealey and Myers, 1996, p. 101).

Since constants can be neglected for optimization, the implied optimization problem is given by:

$$\begin{cases} \frac{\min\left\{F,\sum_i C_i x_i\right\}+\sum_i C_i(1-x_i)}{\min\left\{F,\sum_i R_i x_i\right\}+\sum_i R_i(1-x_i)} \rightarrow \max\limits_{x_i,F} \\ s.t. \quad \frac{F}{\sum_i EAD_i x_i} \in [f_0, f_1] \\ \quad x_i \in [0,1] \end{cases}$$

6.4.5 Objective 3: Optimization of RoE and RoRaC

If information on the adjusted income N_i for each borrower i is available, both traditional and risk-adjusted return measures can be optimized directly. Bluhm et al. (2002), p. 254, give an example for RoE manipulation by securitization under the old capital regime. Their result is based mainly on the observation that under Basle I, credit swaps with certain counterparties have a risk weight of only 20%, and credit-linked notes require no capital.

In comparison to the model in the previous section, the analysis of returns calls for different and additional inputs. Apart from the adjusted income, these include in particular the securitization transaction costs C. Transaction costs include fees for external parties such as underwriters, rating agencies, servicers or trustees. Internal costs are incurred due to the preparation of the relevant information, for example.[63] Such costs are difficult to quantify and can be assumed to be relatively constant for the type of standardized securitization transactions typical for car loans and leases. In this case, they are independent of the transaction's composition, which allows the term in the optimization model to be neglected. The costs should, however, be subtracted from the optimization result to check the true profitability. Otherwise, a function $C(x_i, F)$ must be constructed for the relation between transaction costs and the decision variable. The general optimization problem is then given by:

$$\begin{cases} \frac{\sum_i N_i(1-x_i)-C(x_i,F)}{\min\left\{F,\sum_i R_i x_i\right\}+\sum_i R_i(1-x_i)} \rightarrow \max\limits_{x_i,F} \\ s.t. \quad \frac{F}{\sum_i EAD_i x_i} \in [f_0, f_1] \\ \quad x_i \in [0,1] \end{cases}$$

[63] Rosenthal and Ocampo (1998), p. 231, give an example calculation for the financing costs involved in structuring auto loans.

This model does not involve the calculation of economic capital. Thus, the approximation outlined in section 6.4.1 is not necessary.

The application of the framework to RaPMs is straightforward: the denominator, i.e. regulatory capital, must be replaced by economic capital in the objective function. The optimization problem is then given by:

$$\begin{cases} & \frac{\sum_i N_i(1-x_i)-C(x_i,F)}{\min\left\{F,\sum_i C_i x_i\right\}+\sum_i C_i(1-x_i)} \to \max\limits_{x_i,F} \\ s.t. & \frac{F}{\sum_i EAD_i x_i} \in [f_0, f_1] \\ & x_i \in [0,1] \end{cases}$$

These two problems provide approaches for choosing contracts for securitization which are easy to implement and are in accordance with return-oriented bank management. Since the general setting is based on a simplified transaction structure, it does not take into account the enhancement structure of a securitization. As an example, additional income due to excess spreads, overcollateralization or balances from the cash pool might be relocated to the issuer. This would further increase the total adjusted income. Most of these effects are only one-sided, however, and serve to increase the realized profit. Hence, neglecting them implies a conservative, careful point of view.

6.4.6 Alternative Problem Formulations

For implementation, the models should be reformulated as linear problems if possible. This requires a reformulation of side constraints, and the ratio model for regulatory capital arbitrage. The former can be reformulated as follows:

$$\frac{F}{\sum_i EAD_i x_i} \in [f_0, f_1] \Rightarrow \begin{cases} F - f_0 \sum_i EAD_i x_i \leq 0 \\ F - f_1 \sum_i EAD_i x_i \geq 0 \end{cases}$$

Furthermore, the models for capital arbitrage contain non-linear minimum functions, which can be avoided by splitting the problem in two. From the solutions to these subproblems, the globally best solution must be chosen. Using this approach, the minimum function is replaced by either of its arguments. An additional side constraint must be utilized to ensure that the

Original Objective Function			
$\min\{F, \sum_i R_i x_i\} - \min\{F, \sum_i C_i x_i\} + \sum_i (R_i - C_i) \cdot (1 - x_i)$			
No.	**Alternative Objective Function**	**New Side Constraint I**	**New Side Constraint II**
1	$\sum_i (R_i - C_i) \cdot (1 - x_i)$	$F \leq \sum_i R_i x_i$	$F \leq \sum_i C_i x_i$
2	$F + \sum_i R_i \cdot (1 - x_i) - \sum_i C_i$	$\sum_i C_i x_i \leq F$	$F < \sum_i R_i x_i$
3	$\sum_i R_i - F - \sum_i C_i \cdot (1 - x_i)$	$\sum_i R_i x_i \leq F$	$F < \sum_i C_i x_i$
4	$\sum_i (R_i - C_i)$	$F \geq \sum_i R_i x_i$	$F \geq \sum_i C_i x_i$

Table 6.6: Equivalent Linear Optimization Problem

minimum is really achieved. Thus, since there are two minimum functions, four optimization problems must be solved. In the case of the first regulatory capital arbitrage problem, the additional side constraints and the alternative objection function depicted in table 6.6.

6.4.7 Extensions of the Model

The general model can be adjusted and extended to consider specifics of the individual decision situation. With regard to risk management, concentration risks can be taken into account by setting limits on the exposure to single segments after securitization. A desired risk mix can be specified by giving the percentages of the remaining total exposure allocated to each segment. For this purpose, define an additional set J for the contracts belonging to a sector. Then the relative exposure g_j for a given sector $j \in J$ is given by:

$$g_j := \frac{\sum_{i \in j} EAD_i (1 - x_i)}{\sum_i EAD_i (1 - x_i)}$$

To obtain a certain portfolio composition, the following side constraint can be used:

$$g_j \in [g_{0,j}, g_{1,j}] \ (\forall j \in J)$$

In some cases, the total volume of the securitization transaction is prescribed exogenously. This would, for example, be the case when a captive traditionally structures transactions with similar volumes.[64] The following side constraint takes this into account by restricting the total exposure underlying the securitization:

$$\sum_i EAD_i x_i \in [e_0, e_1]$$

Finally, extensions in the form of additional side constraints are also possible with regard to maturity, exposure or credit quality of the contracts to be included in the securitization transaction. This can be of interest with regard to the requirements set by the rating agencies and investors. As an example, the agencies might require that the underlying assets only include loans of borrowers with a certain credit quality.

6.5 Regulatory Framework

The importance the regulator assigns to securitization can be inferred from the number of publications the Basle Committee has devoted to the subject. In addition to the outline set out in what is meanwhile the third Basle II consultative paper, there have been two working papers on securitization in addition to recent changes in 2004.[65] These revisions have been the result of iterative discussions with the industry, e.g. in the course of the three quantitative impact studies, and have resulted in suggestions which are far less complex and less mathematically advanced than originally outlined.

6.5.1 Alignment of the Model in the Regulatory Framework

To align the model described above with the regulatory framework, the formal model must be classified first.[66] In the context of the Basle II regulatory framework, the transaction described above is a "traditional securitization", where the financial institution serves as "originator".[67] Further, it is assumed that the institution employs the internal ratings-based approach for the

---

[64] See for example table 7.1, p. 126, for the average transaction volumes of DC ABS transactions.

[65] See BIS (2001), (2002), (2003), and (2004).

[66] In the following, the symbol "§" refers to the paragraphs in BIS (2003). The contents of the latest BIS publication on securitization, BIS (2004), are still under discussion and, for this reason, neglected.

[67] (See § 502 and § 507).

Input	§	Description
K_{IRB}	570-574	Ratio regulatory capital to total exposure before securitization
L	593-594	Credit enhancement level of tranche
T	595	Volume of tranche
N	596	Effective number of loans
LGD	597	Weighted average loss rate

Table 6.7: Input for Calculation of Regulatory Capital

calculation of regulatory capital.[68] Since analysis is ex ante, it is assumed that no ratings are available for the tranches. From this follows that the supervisory formula approach ("SFA") has to be applied.[69] It is further assumed that the operational requirements for the recognition of risk transference of traditional securitizations are met.[70] Regarding contractual specifications, the modeling of a first loss piece is a special case of a "credit enhancement".[71] Other contractual and non-contractual specifications, such as early amortization features, implicit support or clean-up calls are neglected.[72]

6.5.2 Inputs for the Calculation of Regulatory Capital for Securitized Loans

The SFA approach requires five inputs from the financial institution, which are described in table 6.7. For the calculation of K_{IRB} for a corporate portfolio, first the regulatory capital

[68] This assumption can be justified by the LGD values implied by the vehicle collateral. These are significantly smaller than those prescribed by the regulator in the alternative standardized approach, and thus preferred by the financial institution. The internal ratings-based approach is described in §§ 567-606.

[69] (See §§ 589-599).

[70] These serve mainly to ensure a true sale of the underlying assets to a special purpose vehicle, see § 516 and § 514.

[71] See § 509 for a definition and §743 for examples.

[72] (See § 508 and §§ 510-512).

must be calculated under the assumption that the portfolio is not securitized. For the bottom-up approach, the regulatory model requires the following modification of the probability of default PD_i:[73] [74]

$$PD_i' = N_{(0,1)}\left[(1-\rho_i)^{-0.5}\cdot N_{(0,1)}^{-1}(PD) + \left(\frac{\rho_i}{1-\rho_i}\right)^{0.5}\cdot N_{(0,1)}^{-1}(0.999)\right]$$

In this formula, $N_{(\mu,\sigma)}$ is the normal distribution function with parameters μ and σ. ρ_i can be interpreted as a measure of dependency between credit defaults. For corporate portfolios, it is given by:

$$\rho_i = 0.12\left(\frac{1-\exp(-50\cdot PD_i)}{1-\exp(-50)}\right) + 0.24\left(1-\frac{1-\exp(-50\cdot PD_i)}{1-\exp(-50)}\right) - 0.04\left(1-\frac{S-5}{45}\right)$$

The last term is a firm-size adjustment for small and medium-sized companies, where $S \in [5,50]$ denotes total annual sales in millions of euros. The term is neglected for companies with annual sales above 50 million euros, otherwise 5 serves as a lower limit for S.[75] The regulatory capital requirements for a corporate exposure i are then defined as follows where LGD_i is the loss given default and the exposure is denoted by EAD_i:

$$LGD_i \cdot EAD_i \cdot PD_i' \cdot [1-1.5\cdot b(PD_i)]^{-1}\cdot[1+(M-2.5)\cdot b(PD_i)]$$

Here the maturity adjustment $b()$ is defined as:

$$b(PD_i) = [0.08451 - 0.05898\cdot\log(PD_i)]^2$$

M is the effective maturity of the contract. If it should not be possible, due to data limitations, to calculate M according to a formula, this factor can be set equal to the nominal maturity in years.[76]

The following calculations refer to the simple securitization structure employed in the model. Additional credit enhancements beyond the first loss piece are addressed only in the

[73]Regulatory requirements for corporate exposures are described in § 241. The maturity adjustments are explained in § 288–294. For the alternate top-down approach, see §§ 574, 334 and 211.

[74]For the risk parameters probability of default PD_i, exposure at default EAD_i, and loss given default LGD_i see section 6.4.1.

[75](See §242).

[76](See § 290).

footnotes. In addition, the calculation of the remaining four parameters is done for the first loss piece only, since the other tranches are assumed to be sold to investors. In this case, using the indicator variable x_i introduced above, K_{IRB} can be calculated as:[77]

$$K_{IRB} = \frac{\sum_i LGD_i \cdot EAD_i \cdot PD_i' \cdot [1 - 1.5 \cdot b(PD_i)]^{-1} \cdot [1 + (M - 2.5) \cdot b(PD_i)] \cdot x_i}{\sum_i EAD_i \cdot x_i}$$

The second parameter L is defined as the ratio of the volume of all subordinated tranches to the total volume of the transaction. Thus, L is equal to zero for the first loss piece since there are no further subordinated tranches. For the calculation of the remaining three parameters, three assumptions are necessary. First, regarding the computation of N it is assumed that, for the portfolio, no two or more contracts are with the same customer. It is further assumed that the transaction is not a "resecuritization".[78] Finally, for the calculation of T it is assumed that the notional amounts are equal to the exposure at default. This assumption can be justified by the observation that car financing contracts usually do not include further commitments such as credit lines or covenants. Then the parameters are computed as follows:

$$\begin{aligned} T &= \frac{F}{\sum_i EAD_i \cdot x_i} \\ LGD &= \frac{\sum_i LGD_i \cdot EAD_i \cdot x_i}{\sum_i EAD_i \cdot x_i} \\ N &= \frac{(\sum_i EAD_i \cdot x_i)^2}{\sum_i EAD_i \cdot x_i} \end{aligned}$$

6.5.3 The Supervisory Formula Approach SFA

For the calculation of regulatory capital, three cases as given in table 6.8 are differentiated, depending on the relation of $L + T$ to K_{IRB}.[79] Deduction requires that regulatory capital be held equal to the total outstanding exposure. In the second case, the tranche is split in two, where the part below K_{IRB} has to be deducted, and the SFA is applied to the remaining part.[80] Since L is zero, because there are no subordinated tranches, the third case can be neglected.

---

[77] For the treatment of credit enhancements in K_{IRB} see §§ 572-573.

[78] (See § 596).

[79] (See §§ 575-577).

[80] (See §§ 589-590).

Case	Condition	Implication
1	$L+T \leq K_{IRB}$	Deduction
2	$L+T > K_{IRB}$ and $L < K_{IRB}$	Deduction and SFA
3	$L+T > K_{IRB}$ and $L \geq K_{IRB}$	SFA

Table 6.8: Capital Requirements for Securitizations

The remaining two cases can be further simplified. If $L+T = T = F \leq K_{IRB}$, capital requirements are simply equal to the first loss piece. On the other hand, if $L+T = T = F > K_{IRB}$ contract splitting is required. According to § 580, however, regulatory capital requirements *after* securitization cannot be higher than *before* securitization. This is reasonable, given that the inherent risk has not been increased by the transaction. Since it cannot be larger than K_{IRB}, regulatory requirement is thus given by:

$$\rho^{Reg} = \min\left\{F, K_{IRB}\right\} \tag{6.1}$$

Chapter 7

Empirical Analysis

This chapter consists of four sections and describes the results from the implementation of the framework set out in the previous chapters. After this introduction, the following section outlines the choice and the implementation of the credit risk model, the general framework, and the different optimization models. It also includes a description of the Monte Carlo simulation.

In the second section, the unique data sources used in this thesis are presented. Data are derived from both public sources and a large German captive. Publicly available is the default rate information published by the Statistisches Bundesamt (Federal Statistical Office). This is employed to derive default rate volatilities and correlations. In contrast, both the loss rate and customer information are derived from the captive's internal sources. Customer information consists in particular of the risk parameters probability of default ("PD") and exposure at default ("EAD").

In the third chapter, the empirical results are presented, including a separate analysis of the risk contributions. The final chapter summarizes and concludes.

7.1 Implementation

7.1.1 Model Choice, Parameterization and Implementation

For the implementation of the framework described in chapter 6 a credit risk model with certain attributes is required.[1] From a modeling perspective it should allow additive risk contributions to be calculated. Moreover, the inclusion of stochastic loss rates and default rate volatility is called for. Finally, the model should be applicable for the type of loan and lease portfolios predominant in the automotive industry, which implies, in particular, parsimony. All these criteria are met by the CR+ extension developed in Bürgisser et al. (2001).[2] This model offers the additional benefit that loss distributions can be calculated analytically and thus very fast.

In contrast to the traditional CR+ approach, the model in Bürgisser et al. (2001) requires correlations and variances for both default rate sectors, and loss rate segments. It does not necessitate, however, the assignment of sector weights. The implementation is further facilitated by assuming that there is no individual loss rate risk driver, i.e. $\delta_i = 0$. Such a parameter would be difficult to quantify; instead loss rate risk is induced exclusively by the stochastic segment scaling factor. Thus, the diversified portion σ^2_{div} of the total loss variance in theorem 3, p. 56, must be adjusted as follows:

$$\sigma^2_{div} = \sum_r \left(1 + \delta^{(r)2}\right) \sum_s \sum_{i \in S^{(s)} \cap L^{(r)}} \left[PD_i - \left(1 + (\sigma^{(s)})^2\right) PD_i^2\right] \epsilon_i^2$$

The deterministic individual loss rates are set equal to the mean of the segment the borrower belongs to.

For the computation of the one sector/segment standard deviation $\sigma^{(s)}$ from the loss variance $V(\widetilde{L})$, the model with only one default rate sector s is chosen.[3] This approach has also been suggested as the first alternative in Bürgisser et al. (2001), p. 17. Thus, the total loss

[1]For the choice of credit risk models, also see chapter 3.
[2]See section 4.3.2.
[3]See section 4.3.2.

variance equation must be solved for $\sigma^{(s)}$:[4]

$$\begin{aligned} V\left(\tilde{L}\right) &= \sum_{i\in I} PD_i \cdot \nu_i^2 + \left(\frac{\sigma^{(s)}}{\mu^{(s)}} EL\right)^2 \Leftrightarrow \\ \sigma^{(s)} &= \frac{\mu^{(s)}}{EL}\sqrt{V\left(\tilde{L}\right) - \sum_i PD_i \cdot \nu^2} \end{aligned}$$

Concerning the mean $\mu^{(s)}$ of the single default rate factor, the original suggestion in Wilde (1997a), p. 37, is taken up. That is, the mean is estimated as the sum of the individual average default rates:

$$\mu^{(s)} = \sum_i PD_i$$

As a final parameterization issue, the standardization unit L is set equal to the smallest net exposure L_i in the sample. The standardized values are rounded up to obtain conservative estimates. All computations are based on these transformed values, which also ensures the nondisclosure of the underlying portfolio.

All implementations, with exception of the optimizations, are done in the free software R.[5] R is a system for statistical computation, in particular providing excellent graphical interfaces. For the solution of the PGF, the approach set out in Kurth and Tasche (2003) is employed.[6] To validate the implied loss distribution, three problem checks are performed to detect subtractive cancellation among other things. First, the sum of all probabilities is equal to one. It turns out that, second, means and variances of the loss distribution match those obtained from the sample. And third, there are no negative probabilities. Since the approach thus seems valid, alternative solutions for the PGF are not further pursued.

7.1.2 Implementation of Framework and Problems

Due to the lack of available information on adjusted income, the optimization of both RoE and RoRaC is not possible. This leaves three problems involving economic and regulatory capital for implementation: two capital arbitrage models and the minimization of regulatory capital.

[4] See equation 5.2, p. 78.

[5] (See R Development Core Team, 2003).

[6] For the derivation of the loss distribution from the probability generating function, see section 4.4.1.

DaimlerChrysler	Original Balance of Tranche (mio)						Subordination (%)
Auto Trust	A-1	A-2	A-3	A-4	FLP	Total	
2000-A	408	655	405	440	74	1,982	0.0375
2000-B	408	620	455	425	74	1,982	0.0375
2000-C	413	625	475	400	69	1,982	0.0350
2000-D	254	550	600	350	59	1,813	0.0325
2000-E	300	790	370	340	60	1,860	0.0325
2001-A	300	790	370	340	61	1,861	0.0325
2001-B	299	615	48	405	60	1,427	0.0306
2001-C	296	695	353	452	60	1,856	0.0325
2001-D	517	600	675	425	74	2.291	0.0325
2002-B	357	675	430	395	62	1,919	0.0312
2002-C	380	700	550	372	67	2,069	0.0326

Table 7.1: Tranche Distributions of DaimlerChrysler Auto Loan ABS (Source: `http://www.ABSNet.net`)

Regarding the side constraints, those additionally suggested in section 6.4.7 are neglected, again due to a lack of information. Moreover, for most of the suggested constraints it is difficult to generally specify intervals which are to a large degree dependent on the individual decision situation. Requirements by the rating agencies, and thus the investors, are hence incorporated exclusively in the first loss piece.

To specify the intervals for the constraints on the first loss piece, an analysis of historical ABS transactions by DaimlerChrylser has been performed. As can be seen from table 7.1, empirical values of the FLP for DaimlerChrysler transactions lie between 3.06 and 3.75%. Thus, the interval $[3.00, 3.75]$ % is chosen for the FLP constraint. Although historical values are relatively constant in this case, it is essential to keep in mind that the setting of the FLP as enhancement is generally a highly interactive and iterative process.

7.1.3 Simulation of Loss Distribution

To validate the approximation of economic capital, the loss distribution after the suggested securitization transaction is simulated. The Monte Carlo experiment encompasses ten thousand runs involving the following steps.

In the first step, a single, gamma-distributed random variable is generated representing the default rate sector scaling factor. Its location and scale parameter are chosen in accordance with the empirical results as derived from the model in Bürgisser et al. (2001).[7] The scaling factor is used in the second step to transform the individual PD_i as assumed in the CR+ model. This step generates the implicit default correlations. High realizations of the random variable, for example, imply high individual default rates. A maximum value of one is then imposed on the transformed values. Using these adjusted default probabilities, Bernoulli experiments are simulated in the third step. If the resulting random variable is of value one, it is assumed that the contract defaults and that the product of the standardized exposure and the loss rate is lost. The borrower automatically defaults if the adjusted default probability is equal to one.

Employing the calculated individual losses for each path, the sums of losses are calculated separately for unsecuritized and securitized contracts. This separation is based on the assignment of contracts derived in the optimization. In the final step, the loss from the securitized contracts is restricted by the first loss piece. Total loss, for each of the simulations, is then computed as the sum over unsecuritized and potentially restricted securitized contracts.

Having generated a sample of 10,000 loss realizations, the risk measures for the calculation of economic capital are estimated by the straightforward estimators suggested in Acerbi and Tasche (2001). Let $(X_{1:n}, ..., X_{n:n})$ denote the order statistics of the simulation sample with dimension n. For a given level of α, further define:[8]

$$\omega = \lfloor n(1-\alpha) \rfloor = max\,(m \in \mathbb{N} | m \leq n(1-\alpha))$$

[7]See section 7.1.1.

[8]In this case, n is given by 10,000, and $\alpha = 0.999$.

Estimators for $\rho^{VaR}(\widetilde{L})$ and $\rho^{ES}(\widetilde{L})$ can then be constructed as:

$$\widehat{\rho}^{VaR}(\widetilde{L}) = X_{\omega:n}$$
$$\widehat{\rho}^{ES}(\widetilde{L}) = \frac{1}{\omega}\sum_{i=\omega}^{n} X_{i:n}$$

7.2 Data Information and Manipulations

7.2.1 Loss Rate Information

Database Description

With respect to loss rates, only residual values are taken into account. In accordance with the results in Schmit (2002), other drivers such as re-collection costs or late payments are neglected. This study finds residual values to be the predominant force in recovery rates. Loss rates are then estimated as one minus the percentage residual value, i.e. the recovery rate. As loss rate segments, a high-level classification scheme consisting of eight segments, numbered from zero to seven, is employed. The classification is a simplified version of the system employed at the captive. For the empirical analysis, residual values from an internal database are used.

The database comprises not only vehicles which have been recollected due to borrower default, but also those which have been regularly returned from lease contracts. Among other, it contains information on the age and type of the car, the new price, and used car prices achieved. The database does not provide information on trucks and other heavy vehicles which are remarketed through separate sales channels. For this reason, utility vehicles are neglected in the analysis. Information is furthermore restricted to the manufacturer's brands, which are sold by traders belonging to the Group. In contrast, most manufacturers cooperate with independent traders, which forbids the availability of an internal database of used car prices.

Calculation of Realized Recovery Rates

As defined in the Basle II requirements, credit risk management is involved with the *economic* loss at the time of default: all cash flows resulting from the default, in particular the resale value of the vehicle, must thus be discounted to the time of default.[9] This induces both general and data-specific problems. A general problem is the question of which yield curve is to be employed for discounting, which should reflect the risks involved in the used car market. Such a yield curve, however, does not exist, and no proxy is available. Moreover, data-specific problems arise around the time of default, which is not available in the database.

These problems necessitate the application of a pragmatic approach concerning both yield curve and time of default, if interest rates are not to be neglected completely. Such a pragmatic approach is to discount each used car value to the time when the new car has been sold, employing an uniform ad hoc interest rate. In this thesis, an arbitrary uniform monthly discount rate of .5 % is employed. Thus, the percentage residual value for vehicle j in the database is calculated by the following formula, where the age $\bar{a}_j$ of vehicle j in the database at the time of remarketing is given in months:

$$RV_j = \frac{\text{Used Car Price}_j}{\text{New Car Price}_j} \cdot \frac{1}{1.005^{\bar{a}_j}}$$

From the realized residual values RV_j, loss rates LGD_j for each vehicle j can be obtained:

$$LGD_j = 1 - RV_j$$

Computation of Model Parameters

The sample of realized residual values incorporates both the effects from the borrower-specific severity $\tilde{l}_i$, and of the segment factor $\tilde{Y}^{(s)}$.[10] As set out in section 7.1.1, $\tilde{l}_i$ is assumed to be degenerate, i.e. $\delta_i = V(\tilde{l}_i) = 0$. Thus, the sample is to be employed to derive the following three groups of model parameters.

- Borrower-specific loss rates $LGD_i^{(r,a)}$[11]

[9](See BIS, 2003).

[10]See section 4.3.2.

[11]This parameter can be interpreted as expected value $E(\tilde{l}_i)$.

- Correlations between segment loss rates $Cor\left(\tilde{Y}^{(r)}, \tilde{Y}^{(s)}\right)$
- Variances of segment loss rates $\delta^{(r)}$[12]

To approximate the age a_i of the vehicle underlying contract i, it is assumed that all contracts have a life-span of 36 months. It is further assumed that the maximum and minimum exposure in each segment r are representative for the exposure in month 36 and month 1, respectively. For each borrower in the segment, the month is then assigned based on a linear interpolation between the maximum and the minimum exposure. The age a_i is also employed to approximate maturities, i.e. remaining contract durations at the time of default, which are required for the calculation of regulatory capital.[13] Given a_i the maturity M_i is derived as: $M_i = min(36 - a_i, 1)/12$. The denominator is required since maturities are measured on a yearly basis, as opposed to the monthly scale of vehicle age a_i.

For the computation of the loss rate LGD_i of borrower i, both the segment r and the age a_i of the vehicle underlying contract i are matched. LGD_i is equated to the mean $\mu^{(r,a)}$ calculated for the same pair of segment and age in the database. If $n^{(r,a)}$ denotes the number of vehicles in sector r and of age a, $\mu^{(r,a)}$ can be computed as:[14]

$$\mu^{(r,a)} = \frac{1}{n^{(r,a)}} \sum_{j \in (r,a)} LGD_j^{(r,a)}$$

The estimation of borrower and segment-specific loss rate parameters considers another criterion in addition to the loss rate segment r and the vehicle age a_i: the time t_j at which a vehicle j in the database has been remarketed. t_j is measured in months and years, vehicle j may for example have been resold in January 1999. For each time t a sample vector of realizations of the segment factors $\tilde{Y}^{(r)}$ is constructed in two steps: first, the borrower-specific component is removed from the sample by standardization; second a multivariate sample is constructed to derive segment standard deviations and correlations.

---

[12]The expected value of the segment loss rates is assumed to be uniformly of value one.

[13]See section 6.5.2. Since the time of default is not available it is set equal to the time of remarketing.

[14]The superscript index (r, a) indicates that vehicle j belongs to loss rate segment r and the vehicle is of age a (in months). Note that age a_i of an underlying vehicle in the portfolio and age $\bar{a}_j$ of a vehicle in the database are set equal.

For the standardization, it is assumed that the effect of age across all vehicles in a segment r at time t cancels out when taking the mean. Thus, vehicle loss rates LGD_j are standardized by the mean loss rate of all vehicles in that particular subset described by a unique combination of r and t. For the construction of the multivariate sample it is further assumed that for each combination (r, t), the loss rates are normally distributed. The elements of each vector are then approximated by the mean of all standardized loss rates in the subset given by (r, t). Based on the sample vectors, the remaining segment parameters, correlations between segment loss rates and their variances, can be computed. The estimators for the different segment loss rates are set out in table 7.2. As can be expected, all correlations are positive. But although most values are significantly higher than 0.8, one is as small as 0.47. Most of the relatively small correlations concern segment 0.

Segment	SD	Correlation with Segment							
		0	1	2	3	4	5	6	7
0	0.397816	1.0000							
1	0.455355	0.6347	1.0000						
2	0.424785	0.5954	0.9125	1.0000					
3	0.602302	0.6751	0.9704	0.9845	1.0000				
4	0.357212	0.6346	0.8756	0.8918	0.9119	1.0000			
5	0.575319	0.4721	0.8159	0.8933	0.9122	0.7880	1.0000		
6	0.705645	0.6360	0.8333	0.8819	0.8996	0.7677	0.8224	1.0000	
7	0.515283	0.5970	0.8397	0.8824	0.8941	0.7728	0.7727	0.7794	1.0000

Table 7.2: Correlations between Loss Rates (Source : Database)

7.2.2 Default Rate Information

Default rate information, given per industry, is taken from the publications of the German Statistisches Bundesamt (Federal Statistical Office). Table 7.3 sets out a short description of the segmentation. The old industry segmentation WZ79, named for its initiation in 1979, was

WZ93	
Id	**Short description**
A	Forestry
B	Fishery (combined with A)
C	Mining
D	Manufacturing
E	Energy and water supply
F	Construction
G	Trade
H	Hotels and restaurants
I	Communications and information transmission
J	Credit and insurance
K	Real estate
L	Civil service, defense, social insurance
M	Education (combined with L)
N	Health care, veterinary, welfare
O	Other public and private services

Table 7.3: Classification WZ93 (Source : Statistisches Bundesamt)

modified in 1994. Since comparability cannot be ensured, only default rates from January 1994 to December 2002 could be employed in the analysis. Moreover, due to the lack of defaults in these sectors, information concerning sectors A and B as well as L and M are combined into one. Figure 7.1 portrays the time series of defaults for four selected sectors: manufacturing (D), construction (F), trade (G), and credit and insurance (J). As can be seen, historical default rates differ between the sectors and display significant volatilities. The default rate information is required to estimate means and variances of and correlations $Cor(\widetilde{X}^{(s)}, \widetilde{X}^{(t)})$ between default rates sectors. Since the model outlined in Bürgisser et al. (2001) requires default rates to be of mean one, the empirical data are standardized by the mean. Based on the transformed

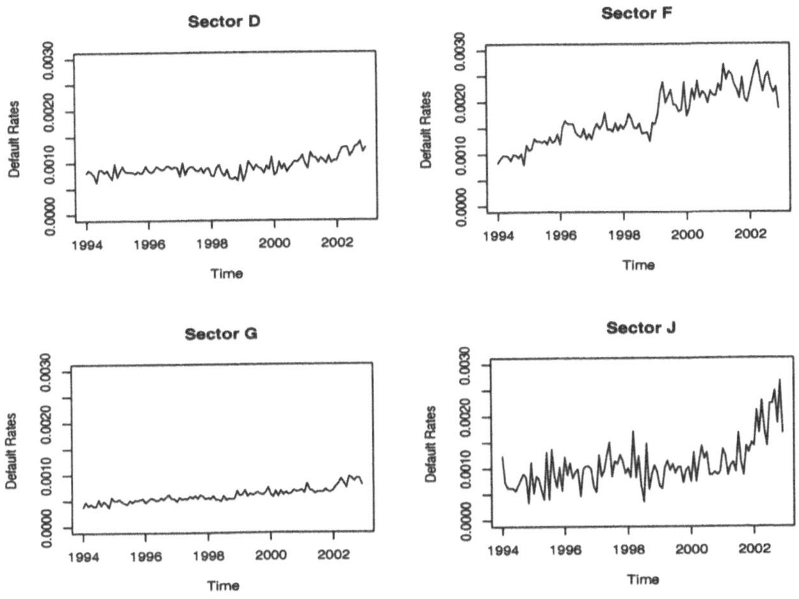

Figure 7.1: 1994-2002 Default Rates for Segments D,F,G,J (Source : Statistisches Bundesamt)

sample, standard deviations and correlations as set out in table 7.4 are estimated. As in the case of loss rate segments, all correlations are positive. The table contains, however, more relatively small values which are even close to zero for the correlation between sectors C and E. This observation concerns, in particular, the mining sector (C), which might be due to data limitations in a rather small industry.

7.2.3 Borrower Information

The empirical analysis is based on an adjusted subportfolio of a captive's corporate portfolio in 2000. The estimation sample contains 14,083 contracts and employs risk parameters prepared in the course of a Basle II impact study. Due to outlined limitations of the database contracts

Sector	SD	Correlation with Sector												
		AB	C	D	E	F	G	H	I	J	K	LM	N	O
AB	0.258041	1.0000												
C	0.895210	0.2761	1.0000											
D	0.174001	0.5709	0.3063	1.0000										
E	1.389706	0.2860	0.0646	0.3957	1.0000									
F	0.291023	0.6966	0.4151	0.7278	0.3657	1.0000								
G	0.210514	0.6689	0.3589	0.8440	0.4322	0.8563	1.0000							
H	0.413133	0.6564	0.3681	0.7810	0.4622	0.9056	0.9142	1.0000						
I	0.283911	0.5876	0.3175	0.8252	0.3804	0.7588	0.8329	0.8391	1.0000					
J	0.418147	0.3962	0.2558	0.6741	0.2670	0.5756	0.7194	0.7048	0.6639	1.0000				
K	0.288759	0.6216	0.3413	0.8749	0.4363	0.8252	0.9242	0.9172	0.8937	0.7499	1.0000			
LM	0.502016	0.3276	0.2613	0.5279	0.2560	0.4189	0.4447	0.4228	0.4320	0.2808	0.4641	1.0000		
N	0.470412	0.5838	0.3634	0.6279	0.3672	0.7488	0.7593	0.7973	0.6983	0.5542	0.7445	0.4357	1.0000	
O	0.367050	0.6146	0.3767	0.7587	0.4774	0.8121	0.8851	0.9067	0.8069	0.6537	0.8657	0.4225	0.7645	1.0000

Table 7.4: Correlations Between Default Rates (Source : Statistisches Bundesamt)

with underlying trucks and heavy duty vehicles have been removed. Also deleted are borrowers that are coded as belonging to private households and government organizations, for which no default rates are available.

For each contract i, the probability of default PD_i, the exposure at default EAD_i, and a key for both the loss rate segment and the default rate sector are available. For the computation of both regulatory and economic capital, the exposures are standardized and rounded up.[15] There is large variation among the exposures, although mean and median are close. This indicates that there are few outliers. The probabilities of default also vary significantly, but the huge difference between mean and median implies that the data are spread less homogenously.

Each borrower is also assigned an individual loss rate by the process outlined in section 7.2.1. Similar to the exposure parameter these display significant variation, but mean and median are close. For the computation of regulatory capital, total annual sales S are additionally required.[16] Since this information is not available, it is ad hoc set equal to 5 million euros, the minimum value prescribed by the regulator.

7.3 Results

7.3.1 Loss Distribution and Risk Contributions

The CR+ loss distribution of the pre-securitization portfolio and the portfolio risk measures are given in figure 7.2. The distribution is smooth and has strictly positive probabilities for losses as high as 50,000 standardized exposure units. The risk measures are also summarized in table 7.5, p. 142.

Two remarks are important concerning regulatory capital. First, the regulator targets the same overall ratio of 8.0% of regulatory capital to exposure for Basle II as under the old regime. Yet the ratio for this portfolio at 3.7% is significantly smaller. Thus, even if the risk is overestimated, at least some mitigating effects have been incorporated in comparison to the previous

[15] For the standardization required in CR+, see section 4.4.2.

[16] For regulatory capital, see section 6.5.2.

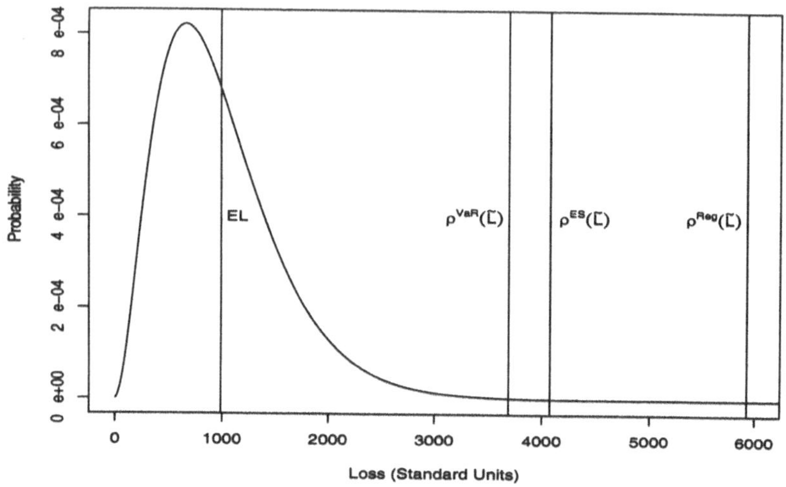

Figure 7.2: Empirical Loss Distribution

capital requirements. These effects should include, in particular, the high recoveries implied by the vehicle collateral.

Second, ρ^{Reg} is larger than both ρ^{VaR} and ρ^{ES}. This result must be put into perspective for two reasons. First, as has been pointed out, data limitations rule out some risk drivers to be contained in the analysis. This concerns, for example, loss-related information such as recollection costs. Moreover, the parametrization involves the employment of multiple mean values, which can be expected to decrease volatilities. With an eye to future and industrial applications, it would be preferable to have vehicle segment indices available for estimation. The effects on the loss distribution and the portfolio risk measures implied by different parameterizations, however, can be significant.

Table 7.5 sets out summarizing statistics for the risk contributions to the following four different risk measures: standard deviation, Value at Risk, expected shortfall, and regulatory capital. Moreover, the expected loss is given by 987. All contributions are additive up to the ninth decimal place. In accordance with regulatory capital calculations, both value-at-risk and expected shortfall are computed at the level $\alpha = 0.999$. The risk contributions to the Value at Risk computed by the approximation suggested in Lehrbass et al. (2001) are not displayed since they do not significantly deviate from those computed using the Euler principle in Kurth and Tasche (2003).[17]

Statistics	ρ_i^{SD}	ρ_i^{VaR}	ρ_i^{ES}	ρ_i^{Reg}
Min.	0.0028	0.0182	0.0201	0.0625
1st Quantile	0.0145	0.0940	0.1038	0.2616
Median	0.0219	0.1420	0.1569	0.3737
Mean	0.0406	0.2628	0.2903	0.4222
3rd Quantile	0.0344	0.2228	0.2460	0.4803
Max.	4.2984	27.7564	30.6685	7.8712
Sum	ρ^{SD}=570	ρ^{VaR}=3688	ρ^{ES}=4074	ρ^{Reg}=5927

Table 7.5: Empirical Risk Measures and Contribution Statistics

On the individual borrower level, risk management analyzes relative, not absolute, risk contributions. Thus, if there is an approximate linear relationship between the individual contributions to different measures, the implications are the same. To check for linearity, a result for the correlation measure can be employed. As shown in Casella and Berger (2002), p. 172, for example, the absolute correlation is equal to one iff there is a linear relationship between the underlying two random variables. This suggests calculating "pseudo-correlations" between the risk contributions, and checking whether they are approximately equal to one.[18] As can be seen from table 7.6, it turns out that there are almost linear relationships between ρ_i^{SD}, ρ_i^{VaR} and ρ_i^{ES}. The relatively smaller correlations of these measures with ρ_i^{Reg}, however, indicate

[17] See section 5.2.2.

[18] Here, the term "pseudo-correlations" is employed since correlations are traditionally computed for samples of random variables only.

different implications from regulatory capital and thus the potential for regulatory capital arbitrage.

For the implementation of the optimization framework, only the risk contributions ρ_i^{VaR} based on the Value at Risk ρ^{VaR} are employed. Although the expected shortfall ρ^{ES} is coherent and hence theoretically superior, ρ^{VaR} is preferred for mainly practical reasons: ρ^{VaR} is the current market standard, and thus more accepted. In this particular case, the choice can also be justified by the insignificant, implied impulses between ρ_i^{VaR} and ρ^{ES} as indicated by the pseudo-correlations.

Risk Measure	**Pseudo Correlation with**			
	ρ_i^{SD}	ρ_i^{VaR}	ρ_i^{ES}	ρ_i^{Reg}
ρ_i^{SD}	1.00000000			
ρ_i^{VaR}	0.99999824	1.00000000		
ρ_i^{ES}	0.99999867	0.99999997	1.00000000	
ρ_i^{Reg}	0.82890490	0.82851540	0.82856870	1.00000000

Table 7.6: Pseudo Correlations Between Risk Contributions

7.3.2 Optimization Results

For optimization, the solver MINOS is employed. MINOS is suitable for large constrained problems with a linear or nonlinear objective function and a mixture of linear and nonlinear constraints.[19] The threshold for the few binary variables not equal to either zero or one is set at 0.5. Thus, only borrowers i where $x_i \geq 0.5$ are contained in the securitization transaction.

As set out in section 7.1.2, for reasons of data availability only three optimization problems can be solved: capital arbitrage concerning both the difference and the index of regulatory and economic capital and the minimization of regulatory capital. With regard to both *arbitrage* problems, the optimal securitization structure provided by MINOS is identical. This indicates

[19] See http://www.ampl.com/BOOKLETS/ampl-minos.pdf.

that the potentially conflicting impulses between the models as discussed in section 6.4.4 do not occur for this particular portfolio. This solution deviates, however, from that for the *minimization* problem.[20]

The optimal solutions to the problems are given in table 7.7. The table sets out information on four aspects: exposure, regulatory and economic capital, and the first loss piece. Included are both absolute values, e.g. the total securitized exposure, and the percentage changes before and after securitization.

Exposure

The solutions suggest that significant portions of the original portfolio be securitized for both the arbitrage and the minimization problems. For the minimization model, only 42.60% of the original portfolio remain in the portfolio, whereas under the arbitrage model the percentage is even smaller at 32.08%.

Economic and Regulatory Capital

The calculation of economic capital by simulation is an issue only for the arbitrage models. Economic capital after securitization is derived according to the simulation procedure outlined in section 7.1.3. The simulated distribution and the portfolio risk measures are displayed in figure 7.3, employing R's default kernel density estimator.[21]

As can be seen in comparison to figure 7.2, p. 135, the tails are less fat, and all risk measures, including regulatory capital, have become smaller. General pairwise relations between the risk measure, however, have been preserved, i.e. $\rho^{VaR}(\tilde{L}) < \rho^{ES}(\tilde{L}) < \rho^{Reg}(\tilde{L})$. It would also seem that the relative distance between regulatory capital and the other risk measures has decreased. This justifies ex post the approximation employed for economic capital of ABS transactions.[22] The expected loss, estimated as the mean of the simulation, has not changed.

The simulated distribution is less smooth than the original loss distribution. Whether this

[20]In the following, the optimization problems are referred to simply as arbitrage and minimization problem.

[21](See R Development Core Team, 2003).

[22]See section 6.4.1.

	Original Portfolio	Arbitrage Problem	Percentage	Minimization Problem	Percentage
Exposure					
Unsecuritized	161,494	51,810	32.08%	68,801	42.60%
Securitized	0	109,684	NA	92,693	NA
Total	161,494	161,494	-	161,494	-
Regulatory Capital					
Unsecuritized	5,926	1,053	17.77%	1,540	25.98%
Securitized	0	3,291	NA	2,781	NA
Total	5,926	4,344	73.30%	4,320	72.91%
Economic Capital (Model and Simulation)					
Economic Capital	3,689	3,090	83.76%	-	-
Regulatory to Economic Capital					
Difference	2,237	1,254	56.04%	-	-
Index	62.25%	71.11%	114.23%	-	-
First Loss Piece					
Size	0	3,291	NA	2,781	NA
FLP/Transaction Volume	0.000%	3.000%	NA	3.000%	NA

Table 7.7: Optimization Results

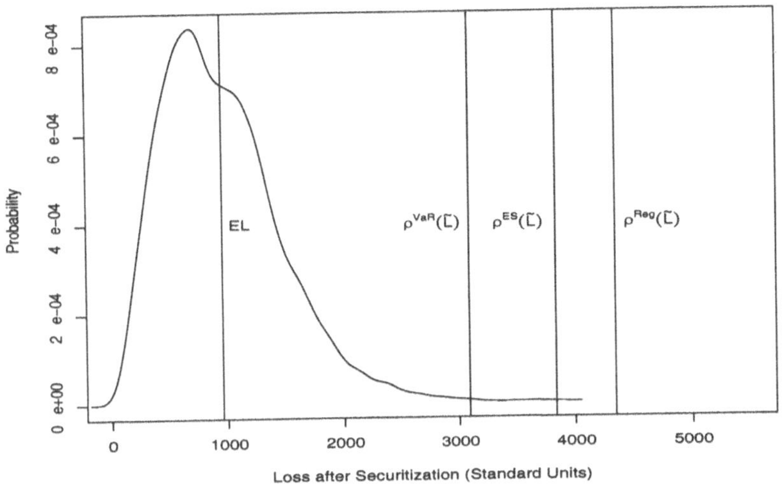

Figure 7.3: Simulated Loss Distribution

is a characteristic feature, or due to either the restricted number of runs or the kernel estimator cannot be determined. This question also indicates the ex post interpretation problems involved in employing simulations.

Generally, due to the incorporation of limits by the first loss piece, regulatory capital has been decreased greatly in both problems. For the arbitrage and the minimization problem they are at only 73.3% and 72.9% of the original amount, respectively. Since regulatory capital has been reduced more sharply than economic capital, both the difference and the index have improved due to securitization. The difference between regulatory and economic capital is at 56.04% only at approximately half of the previous value. The index, i.e. the ratio of economic to regulatory capital, has in contrast been increased by approximately 14% from 62.25% to 71.11%.

First Loss Piece

In both problems, the lower limit of 3% for the first loss piece constraint is utilized fully. Absolute FLP differences are only due to the different securitization volumes of 109,684 and 92,693 standardized exposure units. This can, at least for the minimization problem, be expected from the mechanism through which regulatory capital is restricted by the first loss piece. Since, under the arbitrage problem, the constraint is also fully exploited, the effect must be even stronger on regulatory than on economic capital. That is, the constraint on regulatory capital imposed by the FLP offsets the constraint on economic capital. This indicates again the crucial significance of the FLP for risk management of ABS. Hence, from the issuer's perspective, the FLP should be chosen as small as possible. From the investor's perspective, however, it is also a key enhancement and should be set as high as possible.

Interpretation of Differences Between Solutions

Although regulatory capital requirements are smaller for the solution to the minimization problem, they do not differ much from the arbitrage problems. Moreover, both solutions fully exploit the FLP constraint. However, the unsecuritized exposures under the optimal solutions differ significantly; they vary from 32 to 42% of the original exposure. This implies that there is a non-linear relationship not only between economic and regulatory capital, as indicated by the pseudo-correlations between the risk contributions.[23] Neither are there constant relations between the two capital measures and the exposure of a borrower. This can be expected, since both economic and regulatory capital depend not only on the exposure, but also on loss and default rates. This observation also justifies the employment of a full-blown optimization for portfolio management.

---

[23] See section 7.3.1.

7.4 Conclusion

To summarize, in this chapter three of the securitization models suggested in chapter 6 have been implemented and solved. The implementation utilizes both publicly available and internal information provided by a large captive. Initial results show that there seems to be no significant differences between the relative risk contributions to economic capital across different risk measures such as Value at Risk and expected shortfall. This is, however, not the case for regulatory capital.

Based on the risk contributions, regulatory capital requirements, and further portfolio information, the models are solved. Using Monte Carlo simulation, the approximation of economic capital, if required, has been validated. The results indicate that ABS transactions indeed offer significant potential for both the manipulation of regulatory and economic capital. Even if economic capital is not an issue, asset-backed securitizations allow regulatory capital requirements to be decreased significantly.

Although all three solutions are close there are important differences, e.g. with regard to the securitization volume. These differences could be an indicator that for different portfolios, solutions might deviate to a much higher degree. It also implies that rules of thumb for the choice of securitization portfolios, e.g. based exclusively on exposures, are not reliable.

Chapter 8

Summary and Topics for Future Research

The purpose of this thesis has been to develop a quantitative framework for the choice of contracts for asset-backed security transactions at an automotive captive. Although ABS transactions are used extensively in car financing, risk considerations are usually of less importance than refinancing issues. However, the importance of bank management approaches at captives can be expected to rise in the future. In Germany this trend is driven by the banking status of most captives, which subordinates them under the same regulatory requirements as traditional banks. Regarding the potential for such transactions, it has been pointed out that the captive has different stakeholders with potentially conflicting interests. And it is sales considerations in particular that might lead to huge portfolios of loans and leases whose terms are not adjusted for the inherent risks.

Within a standard ABS framework, where the issuer holds only the first loss piece, different approaches have been suggested. These model regulatory capital arbitrage or risk-return optimization, for example. The approaches have been presented in terms of easy-to-implement optimization problems. With limited additional effort, the problems can be linearized. Multiple side constraints have been suggested, regarding borrower specifics such as maturity, credit score or credit size among other things. Due to data availability and matters of generalization, however, the focus has been on restricting the FLP. The importance of the FLP has also been recognized by the regulator in the setting of capital requirements. In this thesis, the suggested new capital regime Basle II has been implemented.

Since the models also require economic capital contributions as input, the situation in automotive financing has been analyzed to specify an appropriate credit risk model. The result has been the suggestion of CR+ as a model applicable both with regard to the industry situation and under the consideration of the modeling requirements. From the parametrization point of view, the main factor in advance of CR+ is the availability of risk parameters for retail portfolios. Regarding additional requirements, the model facilitates the computation of risk contributions. The observation that CR+ avoids lengthy simulations is also of importance. The application of the model to ABS transactions calls for an approximation of economic capital, which has to be validated ex post by a simulation study.

The parameterization of the model makes use of a unique data set containing both a large captive's internal and external, i.e. publicly available, information. Borrower information is built on a large captive's portfolio containing 14,038 corporate contracts, where data have been standardized for nondisclosure reasons. Loss rate information is based on an internal database of used car transaction prices. Finally, default rate volatilities have been estimated on the basis of publicly available information from the German Statistisches Bundesamt.

The empirical study provides some interesting results. First, there seem to be no significant differences between the relative risk contributions with regard to different risk measures. Measures examined in this thesis were the standard deviation, the Value at Risk, and the expected shortfall. Yet there are differences between the contributions to these measures and regulatory capital for the same contract. This indicates optimization potential the quantification of which has indeed been a result of the empirical study.

Due to limited data availability, only three of the securitization problems could be implemented: these relate to regulatory capital arbitrage and the minimization of regulatory capital. Since no income information was available, the remaining return optimization problems had to be neglected. The optimization results for the two arbitrage models were identical but deviated for the third problem. In all cases, it is indicated that there is significant potential for manipulating both absolute and relative capital figures.

In spite of the unique data sets available for this thesis, several topics for future research evolve around additional information for parameterization. In particular, this concerns loss rates, which Basle II requires to consider all the information concerning economic loss. Practical experience shows the difficulties of assigning controlling numbers such as overhead repossession costs, for example, to single transactions. Parameterization issues can also be expected to be non-trivial when it comes to the computation of adjusted income for the optimization of return on equity and return on risk-adjusted capital, which were not available for this thesis. An important example is the assignment of costs and income to single contracts in the presence of cross-selling.

With regard to an industrial implementation, the framework suggested in this thesis utilizes an analytical credit risk model and can easily be scaled to higher dimensions. At the same time, it is applicable to all finance and lease contracts in car financing regardless of whether these are corporate or retail in nature, and thus to the captive's overall portfolio. The overall potential for credit risk management, however, ultimately will depend on the captive's autonomy granted by the manufacturer.

Appendix: Explicit Calculations for the CR+ Model

Unconditional PGF of Total Losses

The calculation of the unconditional PGF of total losses is a generalization of the calculation for the total number of defaults. The latter can be derived by uniformly setting $\nu_i = 1$. Here, only the PGF of total losses is derived.

Theorem 7 (Lehrbass et al. (2001), th. 2.4) *The unconditional PGF of total portfolio losses in the CR+ model is given by the product over all $A^{(s)}$ given by:*

$$A^{(s)} = \left(\frac{1-\delta^{(s)}}{1-\frac{\delta^{(s)}}{\mu^{(s)}} \cdot \sum_{i \in I} \theta_i^{(s)} \cdot PD_i \cdot z^{\nu_i}} \right)^{\alpha^{(s)}}$$

Proof.

$$\begin{aligned}
A^{(s)} &= \int \exp\left(\left(\sum_{i\in I} \theta_i^{(s)} \cdot PD_i\right) \cdot x \cdot (z^{\nu_i}-1)\right) \frac{x^{\alpha^{(s)}-1} \cdot \exp\left(-\frac{x}{\beta^{(s)}}\right)}{\left(\beta^{(s)}\right)^{\alpha^{(s)}} \cdot \Gamma\left(\alpha^{(s)}\right)} \cdot dx \\
&= \frac{1}{\left(\beta^{(s)}\right)^{\alpha^{(s)}} \cdot \Gamma\left(\alpha^{(s)}\right)} \int \exp\left(\left(\sum_{i\in I} \theta_i^{(s)} \cdot PD_i \cdot (z^{\nu_i}-1)\right) \cdot x - \frac{x}{\beta^{(s)}}\right) \cdot x^{\alpha^{(s)}-1} \cdot dx \\
&= \frac{1}{\left(\beta^{(s)}\right)^{\alpha^{(s)}} \cdot \Gamma\left(\alpha^{(s)}\right)} \int \exp\left(-x \cdot \underbrace{\left(\beta^{-1} - \sum_{i\in I} \theta_i^{(1)} \cdot PD_i \cdot (z^{\nu_i}-1)\right)}_{L}\right) \cdot x^{\alpha^{(s)}-1} \cdot dx \\
&= \frac{1}{\left(\beta^{(s)}\right)^{\alpha^{(s)}} \cdot \Gamma\left(\alpha^{(s)}\right) \cdot L^{\alpha^{(s)}-1}} \int \exp(-x \cdot L) \cdot (x \cdot L)^{\alpha^{(s)}-1} \cdot dx.
\end{aligned}$$

What is left of the integral can now be transformed into a gamma function by substituting $g(x) = u = x \cdot L$:

$$\begin{aligned}
A &= \frac{1}{\left(\beta^{(s)}\right)^{\alpha^{(s)}} \cdot \Gamma\left(\alpha^{(s)}\right) \cdot L^{\alpha^{(s)}-1}} \cdot L \cdot \underbrace{\int_{g^{-1}(0)=0}^{g^{-1}(\infty)=\infty} \exp\left(-u\right) \cdot \left(u\right)^{\alpha^{(s)}-1} \cdot du}_{\Gamma\left(\alpha^{(s)}\right)} \\
&= \frac{1}{\left(\beta^{(s)}\right)^{\alpha^{(s)}} \cdot L^{\alpha^{(s)}}} = \frac{1}{\left(\beta^{(s)}\right)^{\alpha^{(s)}} \cdot \left(\left(\beta^{(s)}\right)^{-1} - \sum_{i\in I} \theta_i^{(s)} \cdot PD_i \cdot \left(z^{\nu_i} - 1\right)\right)^{\alpha^{(s)}}} \\
&= \left(1 - \beta^{(s)} \cdot \sum_{i\in I} \theta_i^{(s)} \cdot PD_i \cdot z^{\nu_i} + \beta^{(s)} \cdot \mu^{(s)}\right)^{-\alpha^{(s)}} \qquad (1) \\
&= \left(\frac{\frac{1}{1+\beta^{(s)}\cdot\mu^{(s)}}}{\frac{1-\beta^{(s)}\cdot\sum_{i\in I}\theta_i^{(s)}\cdot PD_i\cdot z^{\nu_i}+\beta^{(s)}\cdot\mu^{(s)}}{1+\beta^{(s)}\cdot\mu^{(s)}}}\right)^{\alpha^{(s)}} \\
&= \left(\frac{1 - \frac{\beta^{(s)}\cdot\mu^{(s)}}{1+\beta^{(s)}\cdot\mu^{(s)}}}{1 - \frac{\beta^{(s)}\cdot\sum_{i\in I}\theta_i^{(s)}\cdot PD_i}{1+\beta^{(s)}\cdot\mu^{(s)}} \cdot z^{\nu_i}}\right)^{\alpha^{(s)}} \\
&= \left(\frac{1 - \delta^{(s)}}{1 - \frac{\delta^{(s)}}{\mu^{(s)}} \cdot \sum_{i\in I} \theta_i^{(s)} \cdot PD_i \cdot z^{\nu_i}}\right)^{\alpha^{(s)}}
\end{aligned}$$

where $\delta^{(s)} = \frac{\mu^{(s)}\cdot\beta^{(s)}}{1+\mu^{(s)}\cdot\beta^{(s)}}$ and $\mu^{(s)} = \sum_{i\in I} \theta_i^{(s)} \cdot PD_i$. ■

Proof of Recurrence Relation

Theorem 8 (Wilde (1997a), p. 48) *Let a discrete PGF $G(z)$ be of the following functional form:*

$$G(z) = \sum_{n=0}^{\infty} A_n \cdot z^n$$

and assume that the following derivative is a rational function:

$$\frac{d}{dz}\left[\ln G(z)\right] = \frac{1}{G(z)} \cdot \frac{dG(z)}{dz} = \frac{a_0 + a_1 z^1 + ... + a_r z^r}{b_0 + b_1 z^1 + ... + b_s z^s} = \frac{A(z)}{B(z)}.$$

Then this recursion relation holds for the factors:

$$A_n, n \geq 1 : A_{n+1} = \frac{1}{(n+1)\cdot b_0}\left(\sum_{i=0}^{\min(r,n)} A_{n-i} \cdot a_i - \sum_{j=0}^{\min(s-1,n-1)} (n-j) \cdot A_{n-j} \cdot b_{j+1}\right)$$

Proof. From the assumptions follows:

$$
\begin{aligned}
\frac{1}{G(z)} \cdot \frac{dG(z)}{dz} &= \frac{A(z)}{B(z)} \Leftrightarrow \\
\frac{dG(z)}{dz} \cdot B(z) &= A(z) \cdot G(z) \Leftrightarrow \\
\sum_{n=0}^{\infty} [(n+1) \cdot A_{n+1} \cdot z^n] \cdot \sum_{j=0}^{s} b_j z^j &= \sum_{i=0}^{r} a_i z^i \cdot \sum_{n=0}^{\infty} A_n \cdot z^n \Leftrightarrow \\
\sum_{n=0}^{\infty} \left[\underbrace{\sum_{j=0}^{\min(s,n)} (n+1-j) \cdot A_{n+1-j} \cdot b_j \cdot z^n}_{A} \right] &= \sum_{n=0}^{\infty} \left[\underbrace{\sum_{i=0}^{\min(r,n)} A_{n-i} \cdot a_i \cdot z^n}_{B} \right]
\end{aligned}
$$

Two infinite polynomials are equal iff their coefficients are equal. Equating A and B gives the following recurrence relation:

$$
\begin{aligned}
\sum_{j=0}^{\min(s,n)} (n+1-j) \cdot A_{n+1-j} \cdot b_j &= \sum_{i=0}^{\min(r,n)} A_{n-i} \cdot a_i \Leftrightarrow \\
(n+1) \cdot A_{n+1} \cdot b_0 &= \sum_{i=0}^{\min(r,n)} A_{n-i} \cdot a_i - \sum_{j=1}^{\min(s,n)} (n+1-j) \cdot A_{n+1-j} \cdot b_j \Leftrightarrow \\
A_{n+1} &= \frac{1}{(n+1) \cdot b_0} \left(\sum_{i=0}^{\min(r,n)} A_{n-i} \cdot a_i - \sum_{j=0}^{\min(s-1,n-1)} (n-j) \cdot A_{n-j} \cdot b_{j+1} \right.
\end{aligned}
$$

■

Remark 1 *Since $G(z)$ is equated with the total loss PGF, A_n describes the probability of a loss of size n. The initial value A_0 corresponds to the probability of no losses and can be derived as $A_0 = P(Losses = 0) = G(0)$.*

Derivative of the total loss PGF

Theorem 9 (Wilde (1997a), p. 49) *The derivative of the log of the loss PGF without idiosyncratic sector is given by:*

$$
\frac{\partial}{\partial z} [\ln F(z)] = \frac{\partial}{\partial z} \left[\ln \prod_{s \in S} \left(\frac{1 - \delta^{(s)}}{1 - \frac{\delta^{(s)}}{\mu^{(s)}} \cdot \sum_{i \in I} \theta_i^{(s)} \cdot PD_i \cdot z^{\nu_i}} \right)^{\alpha^{(s)}} \right]
$$

Proof.

$$\begin{aligned}
\frac{\partial}{\partial z}\left[\ln F(z)\right] &= \frac{\partial}{\partial z}\left[\ln \prod_{s\in S}\left(\frac{1-\delta^{(s)}}{1-\frac{\delta^{(s)}}{\mu^{(s)}}\cdot\sum_{i\in I}\theta_i^{(s)}\cdot PD_i\cdot z^{\nu_i}}\right)^{\alpha^{(s)}}\right] \\
&= \frac{\partial}{\partial z}\left[\sum_{s\in S}\alpha^{(s)}\ln\left(\frac{1-\delta^{(s)}}{1-\frac{\delta^{(s)}}{\mu^{(s)}}\cdot\sum_{i\in I}\theta_i^{(s)}\cdot PD_i\cdot z^{\nu_i}}\right)\right] \\
&= \sum_{s\in S}\left[\frac{\frac{\alpha^{(s)}\cdot\delta^{(s)}}{\mu^{(s)}}\sum_{i\in I}\theta_i^{(s)}\cdot PD_i\cdot\nu_i\cdot z^{\nu_i-1}}{1-\frac{\delta^{(s)}}{\mu^{(s)}}\cdot\sum_{i\in I}\theta_i^{(s)}\cdot PD_i\cdot z^{\nu_i}}\right]
\end{aligned}$$

■

Theorem 10 (Wilde (1997a), p. 49) *The derivative of the log of the loss PGF with idiosyncratic sector is given by:*

$$\frac{\partial}{\partial z}\left[\ln G'(z)\right] = \frac{\partial}{\partial z}\left[\ln \exp\left(\sum_{i\in I}PD_i\cdot\theta_i^{(0)}\cdot\left(z^{\nu_i}-1\right)\right)\cdot\prod_{s\in S}\left(\frac{1-\delta^{(s)}}{1-\frac{\delta^{(s)}}{\mu^{(s)}}\cdot\sum_{i\in I}\theta_i^{(s)}\cdot PD_i\cdot z^{\nu_i}}\right)^{\alpha^{(s)}}\right]$$

Proof.

$$\begin{aligned}
\frac{\partial}{\partial z}\left[\ln G'(z)\right] &= \frac{\partial}{\partial z}\left[\ln \exp\left(\sum_{i\in I}PD_i\cdot\theta_i^{(0)}\cdot\left(z^{\nu_i}-1\right)\right)\cdot\prod_{s\in S}\left(\frac{1-\delta^{(s)}}{1-\frac{\delta^{(s)}}{\mu^{(s)}}\cdot\sum_{i\in I}\theta_i^{(s)}\cdot PD_i\cdot z^{\nu_i}}\right)^{\alpha^{(s)}}\right] \\
&= \frac{\partial}{\partial z}\left[\sum_{i\in I}PD_i\cdot\theta_i^{(0)}\cdot\left(z^{\nu_i}-1\right)+\sum_{s\in S}\alpha^{(s)}\ln\left(\frac{1-\delta^{(s)}}{1-\frac{\delta^{(s)}}{\mu^{(s)}}\cdot\sum_{i\in I}\theta_i^{(s)}\cdot PD_i\cdot z^{\nu_i}}\right)\right] \\
&= \sum_{i\in I}\nu_i\cdot PD_i\cdot\theta_i^{(0)}\cdot z^{\nu_i-1}+\sum_{s\in S}\left[\frac{\frac{\alpha^{(s)}\cdot\delta^{(s)}}{\mu^{(s)}}\sum_{i\in I}\theta_i^{(s)}\cdot PD_i\cdot\nu_i\cdot z^{\nu_i-1}}{1-\frac{\delta^{(s)}}{\mu^{(s)}}\cdot\sum_{i\in I}\theta_i^{(s)}\cdot PD_i\cdot z^{\nu_i}}\right]
\end{aligned}$$

■

Appendix: Abbreviations

ABS	:	Asset Backed Securities
(D)BET	:	(Double) Binomial Expansion Technique
BIS	:	Bank for International Settlements
CBO	:	Collateralized Bond Obligation
CDO	:	Collateralized Debt Obligation
CGF	:	Cumulative Generating Function
CLO	:	Collateralized Loan Obligation
CR+	:	CreditRisk+
EC	:	Economic Capital
F	:	First Loss Piece
FTM	:	Fourier Transformation Method
IRB	:	Internal Ratings-Based Approach
MBS	:	Mortgage Backed Securities
NPV	:	Net Present Value
PGF	:	Probability Generating Function
QIS	:	Quantitative Impact Study
RaPM	:	Risk Adjusted Performance Measure
RaRoA	:	Risk adjusted Return on Assets
RaRoC	:	Risk adjusted Return on Capital
RoE	:	Return on Equity

RoRaA	:	Return on Risk adjusted Assets
RoRaC	:	Return on Risk adjusted Capital
SFA	:	Supervisory Formula Approach
SPV	:	Special Purpose Vehicle

Appendix: Variables

Default and Loss Rates

j	:	Vehicle in Database
$\bar{a}_j$	:	Age of Vehicle j at Remarketing
t_j	:	Time of Remarketing of Vehicle j
s, t	:	Default Rate Sectors
r, u	:	Loss Rate Segments
RV_j	:	Realized Recovery Rate for Vehicle j
$\widetilde{X}^{(s)}$	:	Default Rate in Sector s
$\sigma^{(s)}$	:	Standard Deviation of $\widetilde{X}^{(s)}$
$\alpha^{(s)}, \beta^{(s)}$	:	Parameters of $\widetilde{X}^{(s)}$Gamma Distribution
$\widetilde{Y}^{(r)}$	:	Loss Rate in segment r
$\delta^{(r)}$	:	Standard Deviation of $\widetilde{Y}^{(r)}$

Borrower Information

i	:	Borrower/Contract
a_i	:	Age of Vehicle Underlying Contract i
I_i	:	Default Indicator for Borrower i
$\tilde{L}_i$	:	Loss from Borrower i
L_i	:	Net Exposure of Borrower i, $L_i = EAD_i LGD_i$
ν_i	:	Standardized Exposure of Borrower i, net of Recovery
ϵ_i	:	Standardized Gross Exposure of Borrower i

EAD_i	:	Exposure at default of Borrower i
$\widetilde{X}_i$	:	Default Probability of Borrower i
PD_i	:	Mean of $\widetilde{X}_i$
$\theta_i^{(s)}$	:	Portion of $\widetilde{X}_i$ assigned to $\widetilde{X}^{(s)}$
LGD_i	:	Individual Loss Rate of Borrower i
δ_i	:	Standard Deviation of l_i

Risk Measures

EL	:	Expected Loss
$\rho^{VaR}(L)$	:	Portfolio Value at Risk, VaR
$\rho^{ES}(L)$	:	Portfolio Expected Shortfall, ES
$\rho^{SD}(L)$	:	Portfolio Variance
$\rho^{Reg}(L)$	:	Total Regulatory Capital
$\rho_i^{VaR}(L)$	:	Contribution of i to $\rho^{VaR}(L)$
$\rho_i^{ES}(L)$	:	Contribution of i to $\rho^{ES}(L)$
$\rho_i^{SD}(L)$	:	Contribution of i to $\rho^{SD}(L)$
$\rho_i^{Reg}(L)$	:	Regulatory Capital Requirements for i

Other

L	:	Standardization Unit
$\widetilde{L}$	:	Portfolio Loss
$C(x_i, F)$	:	Transaction Costs

Bibliography

ABN Amro (2002). Comments on the New Basle Capital Accord. http://www.bis.org/bcbs/ca/abnamro.pdf.

Acerbi, C. and Tasche, D. (2001). Expected Shortfall: a natural coherent alternative to Value at Risk. Working Paper. Available at: http://www.bis.org/bcbs/ca/acertas. pdf.

Albrecht, P. (1999). Risikoadjustierte Performancesteuerung in der Schadensversicherung. In Oehler, A., editor, *Credit Risk und Value-at-Risk Alternativen*, pages 229–259, Stuttgart. Schäffer-Poeschel.

Allen, L., Boudoukh, J., and Saunders, A. (2004). *Understanding Market, Credit, and Operational Risk*. Blackwell.

Allen, L. and Saunders, A. (2002). Cyclical Effects in Credit Risk Ratings and Default Risk. In Ong, M., editor, *Credit Ratings: Methodologies, Rationale and Default Risk*. Risk Books, London.

Artzner, P., Delbaen, F., Eber, J., and Heath, D. (1999). Coherent measures of risk. *Mathematical Finance*, 9:203–228.

Asarnow, E. and Edwards, D. (1995). Measuring loss on defaulted bank loans: A 24-year study. *Journal of Commercial Lending*, pages 11–23.

Berkowitz, J. (2000). A coherent framework for stress-testing. *Journal of Risk*.

Beyer, S. (1996). *Risikomanagement beim PKW-Leasing*. Oldenbourg, München.

Bhattacharya, A. and Fabozzi, F. (1997). The expanding frontiers of asset securitization. In Bhattacharya, A. and Fabozzi, F., editors, *Asset-Backed Securities*, pages 1–20, Chichester. John Wiley.

BIS (1997). *Core Principles for Effective Banking Supervision*. Available at: http://www.bis.org/publ/bcbs30a.pdf.

BIS (1999a). *Capital Requirements and Bank Behaviour: The Impact of the Basle Accord*. Available at: http://www.bis.org/publ/bcbs_wp01.pdf.

BIS (1999b). *Credit Risk Modelling: Current Practices and Applications*. Available at: http://www.bis.org/publ/bcbs49.pdf.

BIS (2000). *Principles for the Management of Credit Risk*. Available at: http://www.bis.org/publ/bcbs54.pdf.

BIS (2001). *Working Paper on the Treatment of Asset Securitizations*. Available at: http://www.bis.org/publ/bcbs_wp10.pdf.

BIS (2003). *The New Basle Accord - Third Consultative Paper*. Available at: http://www.bis.org/publ/bcbsca.htm.

BIS (2004). *Changes to the Securitization Framework*. Available at: http://www.bis.org/publ/bcbs105.pdf.

Bluhm, C., Overbeck, L., and Wagner, C. (2002). *An Introduction to Credit Risk Modelling*. Chapman & Hall, London.

Bodie, Z., Kane, A., and Marcus, A. (2002). *Investments*. McGraw-Hill.

Boegelein, L., Hamarle, A., Rauhmeier, R., and Scheule, H. (2002). Modelling default rate dynamics in the CreditRisk+ framework. *Risk*, September:90–94.

Bolder, M., Lehrbass, F., Lesko, M., and Vorgrimler, S. (2002). Modellierung von Netto-Exposures im Hypothekengeschäft. *Die Bank*, (6):405–409.

Brealey, R. and Myers, S. (1996). *Principles of Corporate Finance*. McGraw Hill, Fifth edition.

Bröker, F. and Lehrbass, F. B. (2001). Kreditportfoliomodelle in der Praxis. In Schierenbeck, H., editor, *Handbuch Bankcontrolling*, pages 773–787, Wiesbaden. Gabler.

Bühler, W. (1998). Risikocontrolling im Industrieunternehmen. In Börsig, C. and Coenenberg, A., editors, *Controlling und Rechnungswesen im internationalen Wettbewerb*, pages 205–233, Stuttgart. Schäfer-Poeschel.

Bund, S. (2000). Collateralized Debt Obligations: Die Formal 1 unter den Asset Backed Securities. *Die Bank*, 3:196–201.

Bürgisser, P., Kurth, A., Wagner, A., and Wolf, M. (1999). Integrating correlations. *Risk*, July:88–93.

Bürgisser, P., Kurth, A., Wagner, A., and Wolf, M. (2001). Incorporating severity variations into credit risk. *Journal of Risk*, 3(4):5–31.

Cantwell, D. (1993). How public corporations use securitization in meeting financial needs: The case of Chrysler Financial Corporation. In Kendall, L. and Fishman, M., editors, *A Primer on Securitization*, pages 55–65, Cambridge. MIT Press.

Casella, G. and Berger, R. (2002). *Statistical Inference*. Duxbury, Second edition.

Christoffersen, P., Hahn, J., and Inoue, A. (2001). Testing and comparing value-at-risk measures. *Journal of Empirical Finance*, pages 325–342.

Cifuentes, A. and O'Connor, G. (1996). *The Binomial Expansion Method Applied to CBO/CLO Analysis*. Available at: http://www.moodys.com.

Cifuentes, A. and Wilcox, C. (1998). *The Double Binomial Method and its Application to a Special Case of CBO Structures*. Available at: http://www.moodys.com.

Cossin, D. and Pirotte, H. (2004). *Advanced Credit Risk Analysis*. John Wiley & Sons.

Crouhy, M., Galai, D., and Mark, R. (2000). A comparative analysis of current credit risk models. *Journal of Banking and Finance*, 24:59–117.

Das, S. (1998). *Credit Derivatives: Trading and Management of Credit and Default Risk*. John Wiley, Singapore.

Debuysscher, A. and Szego, M. (2003). *The Fourier Transformation Method-Overview*. Available at: http://www.moodys.com.

Dentz, M. (2003). Kreditklemme: True Sales Made in Germany. *Das Finanzmagazin für Unternehmer*, July/November:100–101.

Diez, W. and Brachat, H. (2001). *Grundlagen der Automobilwirtschaft*. Auto Business Verlag, Third edition.

Dill, A., Afshar, S., and Carrette, M. (1998). *Auto Lease Securitization: Moody's Rating Approach*. Available at: http://www.moodys.com.

Ernst, Y. (2001). *The Combined Use of Qualitative Analysis and Statistical Models in the Rating of Securitizations*. Available at: http://www.moodys.com.

Fabrikant, B., Becker, K., Bankole, E., and Cotton, C. (1995). *Moody's Approach to Rating Automobile-Backed Securitizations: The Driving Force*. Available at: http://www.moodys.com.

Feuerverger, A. and Wong, A. (2000). Computation of value-at-risk for non-linear portfolios. *Journal of Risk*, 1(3):37–55.

Finger, C. C. (1998). Sticks and stones. Available at: http://www.riskmetrics.com/sticksovv.html.

Finger, C. C. (2001). The one-factor creditmetrics model in The New Basle Accord. *Risk Metrics Journal*, pages 9–18.

Fitch Ratings (2000). *Under the Hood: Automobile Lease ABS Uncovered.* Available at: http://www.fitchratings.com.

Fitch Ratings (2002). *A Road Map to Rating Auto Loan-Backed Securitizations.* Available at: http://www.fitchratings.com.

Frey, R. and McNeil, A. (2002). VaR and expected shortfall in portfolios of dependent credit risks: Conceptional and practical insights. Available at: http://www.mathematik. uni-leipzig.de/MI/frey/rome.pdf.

Gebhardt, G. and Mansch, H., editors (2001). *Risikomanagement und Risikocontrolling in Industrie- und Handelsunternehmen : Empfehlungen des Arbeitskreises "Finanzierungsrechnung" der Schmalenbach-Gesellschaft für Betriebswirtschaft e.V.*, Zfbf Sonderheft 46. Verlagsgruppe Handelsblatt.

Giese, G. (2003). Enhancing CreditRisk+. Available at: http://www.gloriamundi. org/picsresources/gg.pdf.

Gluck, J. and Remeza, H. (2000). *Moody's Approach to Rating Multisector CDOs.* Available at: http://www.moodys.com.

Gordy, M. (2000). A comparative anatomy of credit risk models. *Journal of Banking & Finance*, 24(1-2):119–149.

Gordy, M. (2001a). Calculation of higher moments in creditrisk+ with applications. Available at: http://mgordy.tripod.com/.

Gordy, M. (2001b). A risk-factor model foundation for rating-based bank capital rules. Available at: http://www.federalreserve.gov/pubs/feds/2002/200255/ 200255pap.pdf.

Gouriéroux, C., Laurent, P., and Scaillet, P. (2000). Sensitivity analysis of values at risk. *Journal of Empirical Finance*, 1:225–245.

Gründl, H. and Schmeiser, H. (2001). Risk-adjusted performance measurement in the insurance industry and shareholder value. In *Proceedings of the 5th Conference of the Asia-Pacific Risk and Insurance Association*, Bangalore.

Guthoff, A., Pfingsten, A., and Wolf, J. (1998). Der Einfluß einer Begrenzung des Value at Risk oder des Lower Partial Moment One auf die Risikoübernahme. In Oehler, A., editor, *Credit Risk and Value-at-Risk Alternativen*, pages 111–154. Schäffer-Poeschel.

Haaf, H., Reiß, O., and Schoenmakers, J. (2002). Numerically stable computation of CreditRisk+. Available at: http://www.wias-berlin.de/publications/preprints/846/wias_preprints_846.pdf.

Haaf, H. and Tasche, D. (2002). Calculating value-at-risk contributions in CreditRisk+. Available at: http://www-m4.mathematik.tu-muenchen.de/m4/pers/tasche/ CRplus.pdf.

Hallerbach, W. (2003). Decomposing portfolio value-at-risk: A general analysis. *Journal of Risk*, 5(2):1–18.

Hirtle, B. J., Levonian, M., Saidenberg, M., Walter, S., and Wright, D. (2001). Using credit risk models for regulatory capital: Issues and options. *FRBNY Economic Policy Review*, pages 19–36.

Institute of International Finance (2000). Joint credit risk modelling exercise. Technical report, Institute of International Finance.

Jackson, P., Nickell, P., and Perraudin, W. (1999). Credit risk modelling. *Financial Stability Review*, pages 94–120.

John, K., John, T., and Senbet, L. (1991). Risk-shifting incentives of depository institutions: A new perspective on federal deposit insurance reform. *Journal of Banking and Finance*, 15:895–915.

Jorion, P. (2001). *Value at Risk*. McGraw Hill, Second edition.

Karr, R., Richter, G., Shook, R., and Tsai, L. (1997). Credit-card receivables. In Bhattacharya, A. and Fabozzi, F., editors, *Asset-Backed Securities*, pages 63–83, Chichester. John Wiley.

Kiefer, H. W. (2001). Finanzdienstleistungen im Automobilhandel. In Diez, W. and Brachat, H., editors, *Grundlagen der Automobilwirtschaft*, pages 287–310. Auto Business Verlag, Third edition.

Koyluoglu, H. and Hickman, A. (1998). Reconcilable differences. *Risk*, September(10):56–62.

Koyluoglu, H. and Stoker, J. (2002). Honour your contribution. *Risk*, April:90–94.

Kupiec, P. H. (1998). Stress testing in a value at risk framework. *Journal of Derivatives*, pages 7–24.

Kupiec, P. H. (Winter 1995). Techniques for verifying the accuracy of risk measurement models. *Journal of Derivatives*, pages 73–84.

Kurth, A. and Tasche, D. (2003). Contributions to credit risk. *Risk*, March:84–88.

Lehrbass, F. (2000). Bewertung von Basket-Kreditderivaten und Collateralized Loan Obligations. In Burghof, H., Henke, P., Rudolph, B., Schönbucher, P., and Sommer, D., editors, *Handbuch Kreditderivate*, Stuttgart. Schäffer Poeschel.

Lehrbass, F., Boland, I., and Thierbach, R. (2001). Measuring risk of a loan portfolio using actuarial mathematics. *Blätter der Deutschen Gesellschaft für Versicherungsmathematik*, 10.

Littermann, R. (1996). Hot spots™and hedges. *Journal of Portfolio Management*, 22:52–75.

Lopez, J. A. (2000). An academic perspective on backtesting and stress-testing. Presentation.

Lopez, J. A. and Saidenberg, M. R. (2000). Evaluating credit risk models. *Journal of Banking & Finance*, 24:151–165.

Lugannani, R. and Rice, S. (1980). Saddlepoint approximation for the distribution of the sum of independent random variables. *Advances in Applied Probability*, 12:475–490.

Martin, R., Thompson, K., and Browne, C. (2001a). How dependent are defaults? *Risk*, May:87–90.

Martin, R., Thompson, K., and Browne, C. (2001b). Who contributes and how much? *Risk*, July:99–102.

Matten, C. (2000). *Managing Bank Capital*. Wiley, Chichester, Second edition.

Mazataud, P. and Yomtov, C. (2000). *The Lognormal Method Applied to ABS Analysis*. Available at: http://www.moodys.com.

Meinig, W. (2000). DSFI '99 - Dealer Financing Index. *Zeitschrift für die Automobilwirtschaft ZfAW*, pages 60–61.

Mingo, J. (2000). Policy implications of the federal reserve study of credit risk models at major u.s. banking institutions. *Journal of Banking and Finance*, January:15–33.

Moody's Investors Service (2000). *Historical default rates of corporate bond issuers, 1920-1999*. Global Credit Research.

Norden, L. (2002). Spezialbanken und Basel II: Eine empirische Untersuchung interner Ratingsysteme. *Die Betriebswirtschaft*, 3:273–288.

Ong, M. K. (1999). *Internal Credit Risk Models*. Risk Books, London.

Panjer, H. (1981). Recursive evaluation of a family of compound distributions. *ASTIN Bulletin*, 12:22–26.

Patrik, G., Bernegger, S., and Rüegg, M. (1999). *The use or risk adjusted capital to support business decision making*, pages 243–334. Casualty Actuarial Society Forum, spring edition.

R Development Core Team (2003). *R: A language and environment for statistical computing*. R Foundation for Statistical Computing, Vienna, Austria. ISBN 3-900051-00-3.

Reiß, O. (2003). Fourier inversion algorithms for generalized creditrisk+ models and an extension to incorporate market risk. Available at: http://www.wias-berlin.de/ publications/preprints/817/wias_preprints_817.pdf.

Riess, M. (2003). Value-at-Risk-basierte Bewertung des Restwertrisikos von Pkw-Leasingverträgen. *Finanzbetrieb*, November:725–730.

Rolfes, B. and Broeker, F. (1998). Good migrations. *Risk*, November:72–73.

Rosenthal, J. and Ocampo, J. (1998). *Securitization of Credit*. John Wiley & Sons.

Ross, S., Westerfield, R., and Jaffe, J. (2002). *Corporate Finance*. McGraw Hill, Sixth edition.

Saunders, A. (2002). *Credit Risk Management*. Wiley, New York, Second edition.

Schmit, M. (2002). Evaluation of the expected and unexpected losses of rolling stock leasing business. *Belgian Financial Research Forum*.

Shapley, L. (1953). A value for n-person games, contributions to the theory of games. In Press, P. U., editor, *Annaly of Mathematics Studies*, volume 28. Tucker and Luce, Princeton.

Society of Actuaries (1998). *1986-1994 Credit Risk Loss Experience Study: Private Placement Bonds*. Society of Actuaries.

Standard&Poor's Ratings (1999). *Auto Loan Criteria*. Available at: http://www. standardandpoors.com.

Stuart, A. and Ord, K. (1994). *Kendall's Advanced Theory of Statistics*. Oxford University Press, Oxford, Sixth edition.

Studer, M. (2001). Stochastic taylor expansions and saddlepoint approximations for risk management. Dissertation.

Tavakoli, J. (2003). *Collateralized Debt Obligations and Structured Finance: New Developments in Cash and Synthetic Transactions*. John Wiley & Sons.

Wehrspohn, U. (2002). Bestimmung von Ausfallwahrscheinlichkeiten - Teil 3 : CreditRisk+. *Risk (German edition)*, 9:69–77.

Wilde, T. (1997a). Credit risk+ : A credit risk management framework. Technical report, Credit Suisse Financial Products.

Wilde, T. (1997b). Creditrisk+. In Satyajit, D., editor, *Credit Derivatives & Credit Linked Notes: Trading and Management of Credit & Default Risk*, pages 589–628. John Wiley & Sons.

Wilson, T. (1997a). Portfolio credit risk (i). *Risk*, September:111–117.

Wilson, T. (1997b). Portfolio credit risk (ii). *Risk*, October:56–62.

Deutscher Universitäts-Verlag

Ihr Weg in die Wissenschaft

DUV

Der Deutsche Universitäts-Verlag ist ein Unternehmen der GWV Fachverlage, zu denen auch der Gabler Verlag und der Vieweg Verlag gehören. Wir publizieren ein umfangreiches wirtschaftswissenschaftliches Monografien-Programm aus den Fachgebieten

- ✓ Betriebswirtschaftslehre
- ✓ Volkswirtschaftslehre
- ✓ Wirtschaftsrecht
- ✓ Wirtschaftspädagogik und
- ✓ Wirtschaftsinformatik

In enger Kooperation mit unseren Schwesterverlagen wird das Programm kontinuierlich ausgebaut und um aktuelle Forschungsarbeiten erweitert. Dabei wollen wir vor allem jüngeren Wissenschaftlern ein Forum bieten, ihre Forschungsergebnisse der interessierten Fachöffentlichkeit vorzustellen. Unser Verlagsprogramm steht solchen Arbeiten offen, deren Qualität durch eine sehr gute Note ausgewiesen ist. Jedes Manuskript wird vom Verlag zusätzlich auf seine Vermarktungschancen hin geprüft.

Durch die umfassenden Vertriebs- und Marketingaktivitäten einer großen Verlagsgruppe erreichen wir die breite Information aller Fachinstitute, -bibliotheken und -zeitschriften. Den Autoren bieten wir dabei attraktive Konditionen, die jeweils individuell vertraglich vereinbart werden.

Besuchen Sie unsere Homepage: *www.duv.de*

Deutscher Universitäts-Verlag
Abraham-Lincoln-Str. 46
D-65189 Wiesbaden

GPSR Compliance

The European Union's (EU) General Product Safety Regulation (GPSR) is a set of rules that requires consumer products to be safe and our obligations to ensure this.

If you have any concerns about our products, you can contact us on ProductSafety@springernature.com

In case Publisher is established outside the EU, the EU authorized representative is:

Springer Nature Customer Service Center GmbH
Europaplatz 3
69115 Heidelberg, Germany

Batch number: 10725993

Printed by Printforce, the Netherlands